By *WALTER LOWENFELS*

IN A TIME OF REVOLUTION

Poems from Our Third World

IN A TIME OF

Poems from

Edited by

REVOLUTION

Our Third World

WALTER LOWENFELS

VINTAGE BOOKS
A Division of Random House
New York

VINTAGE BOOKS EDITION, 1969

Copyright © 1969 by Walter Lowenfels

All rights reserved under International and
Pan-American Copyright Conventions.
Published in the United States by Random House, Inc., New York, and
simultaneously in Canada by Random House of Canada Limited, Toronto.

Library of Congress Catalog Card Number: 69-16465

Thanks are due to the following
for permission to use material already copyrighted:
"Benediction" by Bob Kaufman from *Solitudes Crowded with
Loneliness*. Copyright © 1961 by Bob Kaufman. Reprinted
by permission of New Directions Publishing Corporation.
June Meyer for "If You Saw a Negro Lady" from *Poems*.
Copyright © 1968 by June Meyer. Reprinted by permission.
"Visiting a Dead Man on a Summer Day" by Marge Piercy from
Breaking Camp. Copyright © 1968 by Marge Piercy. Reprinted by
permission of the Wesleyan University Press. David Henderson
for "Elvin Jones Gretch" Freak (Coltrane at the Half-Note")
from *Felix of the Silent Forest*. Copyright © 1967 by
David Henderson. "I, Too, Hear America Singing" by
Horace Julian Bond. Copyright © 1967 by American Dialog.
"Goodbye Hkrumah," by Diane di Prima, "Peyote Poem" by
Al Fowler and "Poem for Ernie Henry," by Gloria Tropp
were published in *Intrepid*. Copyright © 1966 by Intrepid.
"Blues for Lucifer" by Marvin Jackman appeared in *Journal
of Black Poetry*. Copyright © 1966 by Journal of Black Poetry.
"Flower Passion" by Tuli Kupferberg appeared in *Wormwood Review*.
"Summary" by Sonia Sanchez first appeared in the *Transatlantic
Review*. "Word Alchemy" by Lenore Kandel is reprinted by
permission of Grove Press, Inc. Copyright © 1960,
1966, 1967 by Lenore Kandel.

Twenty-one of the poets in *New Jazz Poets* have read
their poems in a record of the same title, edited by
Walter Lowenfels and published by Broadside Records, N.Y
Copyright © 1967 by Broadside Records, Inc.

Designed by Andrew Roberts

Manufactured in the United States of America

EDITOR'S ACKNOWLEDGMENTS

To the Rabinowitz Foundations, for the generous grant which helped to make the project for this book a reality.

To Nan Braymer, my collaborator in this, as in all my other work.

To Lillian, my wife, for help and judgment in every stage of the book.

To Ishmael Reed for his help in finding some of the poets.

To Allen De Loach, Editor of *Intrepid*, for his critical judgment and pioneering work in the jazz poetry field.

To Marion Klugman and Manna Perpelitt for their typing.

PROLOGUE

A poem is a word machine that sets each of us up as a new job for a split second. This is the moment that puts the reader's life in the hands of someone who knocks the gibberish out of it and answers the eternal question: *what time is it?*

If you find this hard to grasp today, consider another time, the age of Homer, for example. Where do you turn to but Homer? Or to Shakespeare and Marlowe for the Elizabethan Age; to Michaelangelo and Leonardo for the fifteenth-century Renaissance? Each poet gives you more than his age, but it is only through his particular verbal texture that he transcends its limitations and shows you the clock that never stops. Thus, the poet's art of words, not as evasion of reality but as oral revelation—that it exists and can be lived.

As soon as we read the way Whitman says it: "I contain multitudes," or Clarence Major: "Black heart builds against broken fury," we recognize we knew this before, only it took the man from Brooklyn or Georgia to make it explicit, speak the unsayable in the lingo of his time. "We live inside circles of ourselves" (Emerson) The essential framework around us is always in danger of escaping our grasp because it's in the next degree of vision. It's that degree the poet spells out for us now, today.

All our emotions are different in the 1960's because of what happened in Hiroshima in the 1940's. The words are no longer the same with strontium-90 in the air. This is the inescapable framework for all our lives, all our poems. Not that every poem is a poem about peace and war; on the contrary, "every poem is a love poem." What differs is the essential framework that surrounds the poem—as it does our lives.

On the one hand, the possibilities for disaster seem to get worse and worse; on the other, the possibilities for victory seem greater and greater. As the tensions grow, the number and quality of new poems increase geometrically. Now everybody wants to say his last words, paint his last pictures, write his last symphony. But the very act of writing it down while we can is a sign of belief in tomorrow.

Does it matter? Does it make any difference? Maybe not to the President of Peaceful H-Bombs, or the Secretary of Annihilation. All the poem can do is give us a momentary dilation of our vision. Once you get that wider angle, other things will also relate differently—not all the time perhaps, but in those moments when you are most aware of being alive. So, people write love poems not at the moment of kissing but later, to get into words that endure the instant touch that is otherwise gone so rapidly.

None of this will by itself save the world, and all our kisses, from being blown to hell. What we are talking about is the enormous value of that instant of being alive that the poem spells out for us, and thus in its way helps us to fight for life whenever and wherever we can. Remembering that not to know and love the tragedy of your own life is not to know the joy of being here at all.

It is within this framework that *In a Time of Revolution* was conceived one evening when I attended a reading by Afro-American poets at a meeting of the Poetry Society of America. I had read or listened to most of them before, but hearing them in the shrine of the iambic pentameter sharpened my feeling that their poems had content and sounds that placed them in a special category. I decided to bring together a group of poems that in structure, linear beat, jumps and stops and starts, seem parallel to what a performance by Archie Shepp or John Coltrane achieves in music.

We have in this book a unique development of modern sound that is adding a new dimension to North American prosody, one that goes beyond much of the poetry being recited in this country as well as in the Soviet Union and elsewhere. In today's poetry world there are many circles and some are moving very rapidly. While certain audiences are catching up to what was done in San Francisco in the mid-fifties (the so-called "beat" poets), the current scene has already moved around the time corner.

And yet these are not the "voices of the future," they are the voices of the present. "It is not that the avant-garde artist is ahead of his time, but that most of the rest of us are behind our time."*

Some of the influences reflected in these poems include street rhythms, rock and roll, as well as atonal music and the zoom of the rocket age—counterpointing the special horror and love we are living through in the nineteen sixties. In Polynesia, Africa and elsewhere, tribal traditions are often transmitted generation to generation by chants and dances. The tonal quality, inflections and drum beats have particular references. So these poems represent their own kind of oral history, telling people of our time and future generations what was actually cooking in a phrase like "the long, hot summer."

The poems are not just sound happenings—many of them come out of the guts of people whose excitement, frustrations, terror and revolt have been heard in Watts and Mississippi; on campus and in peace movements rather than in literary circles. The modern horrors are in these poems as well as the cool vision you find in that vast creativity known as The Movement.

I have not, of course, been able to gather together all who may belong in the group, but I believe the collection is representative of what is going on. It was Afro-American poets who started me on this project, but once it got going I added white poets who seemed to me to be swinging.

One of our poets. Calvin Hernton, is a sociologist as well as a poet. Here is a portion of a taped interview I made with him:

"The word elements that make up the symbolism and the metaphors in these poems are drawn from the secular existential experience—not only of the Negro, but of men and women today in general. For instance, my poem 'Jitterbugging in the Streets' came out of the experience Ishmael Reed and I went through during the Harlem riots. Some of the things in the poem literally happened; some

*Edgar Varese

of the dialogue records what a fourteen-year-old kid was actually saying.

"When I wrote, 'There's terror in Harlem, terror that shakes the foundations of the very assholes of the people,' I was trying to get down how terrible the people were feeling; how terrible their conditions were. We use specific terminology as far as the language can carry us today. This may result in forcing upon the reader the reality of a situation, rather than the poetry of it—even though we use poetry to get at actuality.

"What I do is to strive to get a coherence within seemingly contradictory connections. As a farfetched example—to take that typewriter and rearrange its parts in such a way that it's no longer a typewriter but perhaps a motor scooter. Maybe no one could see that typewriter as a motor scooter until I had finished with it, with the creative insight, or what have you, to rearrange its parts. Or think of hammering something into a daisy. A daisy's a very tender thing. Now you're going to hammer and then the daisies become the characters that explode the sun.

"I haven't really probed into why this is so, but I think a case could be made—maybe it comes out of being Negro—I mean being a whole Negro, the experience, not just the accident of being black. I have a notion that the power of the secularity of our poetry is in large measure indebted to the ecclesiastical side of rural life of the Negro. The force in this comes from a deep spirituality—however you define it. It can have something to do with religion—or with the universal, the essence, the intangible soul. So I don't think one can make a mechanical analysis of this kind of poetry, because it isn't written mechanically; it's written out of the heritage which becomes a working tool with a meaningful place in reality. It's a great reach-out to people."

If I seem to white readers to be exaggerating the role of black people in the current poetry upsurge, it may be because in our country black poets have not yet been admitted into the general literary fraternity the way black prose writers have. One thing wrong about the image most white people have of poetry in the U.S.A. is its color. It's almost purely white. This discrimination affects all poets. It sets up a pseudo-standard of what white poetry is in the U.S.A. This can be a fatal blow at our literary judgment, because it leaves out of critical consideration the contributions of the Negro to our poetry and our culture.

What are the facts? The most widely used current anthology, the one edited by the late Oscar Williams, has no Negro poets. That exclusion is true for most other anthologies. Occasionally you find one that has token representation—Langston Hughes or LeRoi Jones. Louis Untermeyer's anthology contains three Negroes from the days of the Harlem Renaissance.

To try and cope with this false image of U.S. poetry, there was the 1949 anthology *The Poetry of the Negro.* Then, after an interim of fifteen years, two anthologies of new Negro poetry appeared, one edited by Langston Hughes and the other by Arna Bontemps. The discrimination is so bad in this country that two anthologies and collections of Negro poets are available only in England, one edited by Dr. Rosey Pool, the other by Paul Bremen. Thus we find that whereas the novelist who is Negro cannot be omitted from any consideration of American literature, there is almost no image of the Negro poet in the English courses in most white universities, or in the standard critical works.

What is it that keeps Afro-American poetry away from most white readers' eyes? A key problem lies in its national or ethnic quality. Although poets like David Henderson or Clarence Major write about many subjects, they cannot help incorporating a special quality into their work that arises out of their special experience as black people in a white country. Thus their work often achieves a verbal texture that is unique. It has roots not only in the world literary traditions from which white poets take off, but also in the oral traditions of black people; their music, their songs, their special way of speaking to each other. It is the experience behind the poem as well as its language that the white reader often rejects as "poetry"; it doesn't seem to fit into the pattern of what white poets have established as the standard of excellence in the U.S.A.

The overall failure of white readers, critics, teachers, anthologists to recognize the role of the Negro poet in the image of American literature is part of the overall white refusal to recognize the image of the Negro in American life. Because it is in essence their national spirit that finds expression in Negro poetry.

This recalls what Whitman said in his later years: "Really great poetry is always (like the Homeric or Biblical canticles) the result of a national spirit and not the privilege of a polished and select few."

I am positive that the image of the poet in America is not lily-white, any more than it is pure black—it is the voice of all of us singing, not in unison, but in our own particular way. And the Afro-American way cannot be denied without denying our country.

LeRoi Jones has written about it, and I quote with his permission: *"HOW YOU SOUND??* is what we recent fellows are up to. How *we* sound; our peculiar grasp on, say: a. Melican speech, b. Poetries of the world, c. Our selves (which is attitudes, logics, theories, jumbles of our lives, & all that), d. And the final . . . The Totality of Mind: Spiritual . . . God?? (or you name it): Social (zeitgeist): or Heideggerian *umwelt.*

"MY POETRY is whatever I think I am. (Can I be light & weightless as a sail?? Heavy & clunking like black boots.) *I CAN BE ANYTHING I CAN.* I make a poetry with what I feel is useful & can be saved out of all the garbage of our lives. What I see, am touched by (CAN HEAR) . . . wives, gardens, jobs, cement yards where cats pee, all my interminable artifacts . . . *ALL* are a poetry, & nothing moves (with any grace) pried apart from these things. There cannot be closet poetry. Unless the closet be wide as God's eye."

WALTER LOWENFELS

CONTENTS

IN A TIME OF REVOLUTION

Poems from Our Third World

Daisy Aldan

Yorkville

Why do you drag me back to Piranesi's *Prisons*
where cats slink around Ruppert's copper Beer vats;
to the stink of cabbage and dust stagnant in the hallways;
the plastic dishes, the oil cloth, the torn window shades;
to the candy store where the clanging clans gather,
the sadists; to the screaming sirens of fire and
                                        ambulance?

I have circled the globe in search of elegance,
heading in the opposite direction to Yorkville,
but you keep tugging that cord tied to my navel,
and here I am hauled, resisting, into the gutter,
and I sprawl over the cracked corpse of my old school
and the yard where the swing-trestles stand like gallows
against the obscenities scrawled on the fractured walls.

Die, will you! and let me forget the paper funeral wreaths.
let them erase the stairways with their concealed
                                        nightmares,
and blast the Irish bars with stale drink stench.
and the German taverns with their *Community Sings:*
and smash the store-window brides and bridesmaids;
                                        dynamite
the Thrift Shops crammed with cast-off garments of the
                                        blighted!

Or am I doomed to hover over hideous Yorkville.
going mad with the rattling of the razed Third Avenue El?

Bob Allen

Musical Vietnams

A polyphonic symphony of napalm bombs
　sounds a melody of busted babies
　　　　　　　　　　　　gutted mothers
　　　　　　　　　　　　　decapitated men
Harmonizing bombers in azure skies
　paint paddies below blood red
　　　　　　　　　　　　bone white
　　　　　　　　　　　　　dead blue
The rhythm of clattering M-14s
　reacts with local citizens
　　　　　　　　　　　　adding further color
　　　　　　　　　　　　to the local scene
This swinging symphony of sound and sight
　is the greatest yet performed by the
　　　　　　　　　　　　　　Great Society
"But who can really dig that jazz
9,000 miles away?"
Don't sweat it man let me clue you in
　　There is a combo in Watts
　　and a quartet in Harlem
　　　rehearsing groovy sounds
　　　　　　　for a spectacular jazz blast

　　　　　　　　　　　right in your
　　　　　　　　　　　back yard

Chant for Half the World
(for LeRoi Jones)

The women as richness of liquid chocolate
between their legs beneath their navels
The women like their own shrieks
glass curse of their angular legs
"in the way the women move" in agony in
graceless flounderings on the smooth
dance floor of their lonely manipulations

The women in their floured eyes
their skin mansions such gifts finally slipped
over inner eyes till fur grows
into the fake charity of the yoni

First girlchild becomes servile
Second loses its birthright escutcheon
Third girlchild has no face fourth is shadow
first girlchild leads schools
second becomes maker of delicate symbols
third creates old specific buttons
fourth is the voiceless farmer's wife

Women with their liberal blackened teeth
moving on round beds above oracies
under stone men as idols of themselves
High priestesses of unnamable objects
called miscarriages of beetroots
Teeth gapped to equal each child lost
Each lost child never bridged

The women breast to breast across empty
across lava-strewn bitter plains
facing lidless eyes of the majestic surgeons
who demand they empty their wombs
of the quintuplet dolls shaped like "husband"
Women offering full teats to
men with infant faces who drink with mouths
the violet of sleep or of healed circumcision

The women their flowing words of casuistry
tennisballs stuffed into mouths

pingpong balls into eye sockets
volleyball up anus marbles in earcurves
nostrils filled with buckshot
Words falling like terrible stars from the yoni

What does she say how gesture like silk
how shed skin in the burn of his piercing
how bend how move between rooms like shoji

Sound of brrrrutsss brrrrutsss smooth
as skin under birch branches of the sauna
"to make the skin glow"
or Lord Sir King Masoch robed advancing
toward la marquesa Mademoiselle de Sade
exchanging vows and blows
The women near men in thick dance forgetting
honey in joints in hollow of bones
of cunt eyes furred away from how it was
with limbs not wooden but la belle sauvage
The forgetting forgotten
across inflamed glass dancefloors
Laughter a bite of betel teethmarks
hair into oiled peaks as foretold
away from false minuets away
from degradation of beet lingam
shined and polished beyond identification

Man reach for me i am firm open i am
waiting in the dark place which has
all secrets i have
have lust as deep as you can reach
But take off that skin that hair shirt
choose between forks of tongue
or is it a forked prick you speak to me with

The women as kosmotics
wombs tipped crazily toward the source light
careening toward the meteorite of fuck
Words of the recent typical distorted poet

gone into words and fat lyrics
behaving like a giant bearded night seed
which refutes its genes assaying day
Saying moon is man sun is woman
Ah better to be content as bucolic barley
than to outguess the sex of planets

Tragedies of women their toothlessness
having had the wombs wormed like sick kits
having little to do but notice how hills
recall flesh as it might have been
Having been bound from infancy to boards
which at other times held their own roast flesh
ready for the obsidian knives

The accurate synaptic traceries prohibited
turned instead into lightning on film
overexposed and comically brilliant

Position of woman in relation to a tree

If you do it against a tree and it is with love
it is as valid as between silk coverlets
he once told his classroom of Vassarites
and was fired for illuminating fifty gates
Or Agnes de Mille leaping in a dark church
given over now to bowings and deep genuflections
antithesis of the good fuck or dance
All the women gone into black for a pope
trained to despise half of humanity

The women walking with eyes turned inward
their fine navels cabbages of joy
along streets paved with vegetables
The women moving seeded and buttered

offering packaged suicides to young men
harnesses cut from the Fallopian Tubes
tied with deaths of their fathers

The rich women of animalskins
waists slanted in memory of wellsprings
stained with sun with come with breastmilk
The women coppered and grafted into love
reaching smiling toward the lingam
The women with blood with liquid chocolate
shrieking letting loose hand and hair
The women walking as memory of man

Winter 1963-4

Art Berger

March on the Delta

One more March
unrolls eyeballs
with scald of scenes
that are dues paid
for space to live;
the eagle flies high
over Mobile as the wind
prays in the street
and a tear gas fog
washes Selma faces
in oxides of nowhere
as we skip double dutch
in space and show
those Russians while
stars fall on Alabama.

One more March
of whirlyhawks over Mekong
sow a notquitelethal
smog of maggots
drooled from lips
of pentagon lunatics
on a defoliate scene
where a lone leaf sighs
a final spring
to a listless world
where lollypop logistics
cinder babies in
napalm gardens
as our face is saved
tho the fig leaf is gone.

The Old Days

The Stupid indelicacy and

roughhouse—the frontier, the pioneer?—That's
how I want to live, fight, drink
laugh, shit al fresco, pee
on the base of a pine tree
watching the limb above for
cats, or sunlight thru them—

To make love with the eyes across
a rude room and
whatever happens after, let
that happen too, like maybe
            push down the door

Fall endlessly drunk on the floor
or range, as wolves in the mountains
far enuf away to keep from getting shot
and close enuf to eat once in a while. No,

that life was not
sweet.
Only possible   /   and sometimes
                        true.

I Too Hear America Singing

I too hear America singing
But from where I stand
I can only hear Little Richard
and Fats Domino
But sometimes
I hear Ray Charles
Drowning in his own tears
or Bird,
Relaxin' at Camarillo
or Horace Silver, Doodlin'
Then I don't mind standing a little longer.
Look at that gal shake that thing
We can't all be Martin Luther King.

Grace Butcher

(sun)day

grass
textures
my naked body

dandelions
pattern
my buttocks

and 4-leaf clovers
criss-cross
my calves

the sun
as heavy
on my breasts
as any lover

knows my thighs
with utter completeness

melts my edges
into the earth

fire leaps
in closed eyes

HA!
and a puff
of dandelion smoke
for the insignificance
of loneliness!

the grass is cool
and writes itself
on my nakedness

and the sun
reads me

with your strong hands

To an African Goddess

to an african goddess
        pubic too small purple sweater
            knees ! cornrows ! pout !
                    yes !
    with weird man-talk of universal image
            you ! who ARE universe !
inspiration actual prostitute of a whole fucked race
                                —orgy of the self made holy
        rape of my whole black mind !
        snug in its unawareness . . .

        young soul-womb
                        sister
        who are my mother
    endless as she is
        with hot iron and flowered dress

                            (! now shoe long !
        like, maybe we can trick a trench coat
        (cold life
                in absolution of all sin
        for your beauty escapes you . . .
beat woman, black madonna black

                tired eyes lie
                scream ! your life was a lie !
                        hand-me-down hoe—
                the soul-womb grown old
        of rag green coat, dues !
                the sweet illusion of wine
                    the hour the doorway
                your womb that has no beginning
                love and endless
                    my wild african goddess

                    mother of the sun . . .

From 21A

no. 2

i am a fish
on a mountain top
i shall line the eagle's nest
          with sea weed
and learn to swim the air
               i shall not perish
               i shall excel
i shall listen for the sounds of the sea and wonder
               how long can the eagle fly
               without a resting place

and taking a deep breath of water
from his sea scout canteen
he opened his fins
and flew into a double dense cloud
suddenly feeling landsick

emerging from the cloud
refreshed by condensation
with well-manicured scales
reflecting more than a light
holding a manmer
          (head half fish ass half man)
holding this manmer
               in his fin pit
he sang a mountain fish version
of a civil rights cloud shanty
ridiculing the marcelled hair around
the manmer's dorsal fin
checked the manmer's gills for mountain dew
strapped on his air mask
and swam away to his
sea weed lined eagle's nest
mumbling in his bubbles about
                    assimilation

strung out without hope
hung up without rope
undone and done in

this callused coat of scars called skin
is ready for the ragbag
my head is my Achilles heel
hard hat and helmet may
protect it from the bat and hatchet
but my eyes and ears are always open

my head is a mountain spring
my spine is a young river
a thousand tributaries flow
to beat against the sea walls
of my finger tips

my head is an unfaithful geyser
scalding the back of my eyes
no fish live in my river
only rusty rivets from dead battleships

my head is a whirlpool
in the mouth of an erupting volcano
i can neither cave in nor explode
i am stable

my eyes and ears always open
where is the oil for my troubled waters
whirlpool sucking volcano erupting
where is my safety valve
i'd better close my eyes and ears . . . just a little
perhaps........i'll almost sleep

Nation

In the furrows of the world
the paths of planting
the hoe-trails of our people

Among the cotton white
between the stalks of sticky cane
deep in sweltering diamond holes
in the wash of salty sweat

inside:

* tobacco roads,
  the shanty towns,
  packed, in ghetto stacks

In jungle bush
and Whitey's kitchens

Backs unbend
and bodies stretch

Muscles that made the world begin to flex.

We
would be
what we can do

Engaged in struggle
today and
            yesterday

People!

black, yellow, brown
around the world
around the golden sun
We!

can only be
do
from what we are.

II.

Our hands have clenched hammers, hoes, and hope

Our backs have broken ground

around
the world

Our cries have crashed through terror
torn nights

Our bodies burnt
      the earth a bitter black

To rise

in
anger. *pause*

And I suppose
it *hold*
   will come
someday,

this thing
this black I am
that has to battle now *to be* ⟶

to
be

We will not have to say

someday,

nor fight
for what we are.

We! will be

simply
be,

We.
My children

or
   my
      children's
children

will know

We
  (are of roots
long, strong,
roots) which
grew into the world!

We!

the tree

seeds
we

spread

take root

grow *high*

and my children shall know.

(meanwhile I) Search
words for:

Nation
Strength
People
       (now)

Chorus for Phonograph

Fine weather boosts holiday traffic toll,
an all-time record for the world.
I have a headache. Do not incinerate.
Why don't you go out and play with the other boys?
Cut along the dotted line. To remove, pull tab.
In case of emergency,
lift arm. Pull up. Push out.
Carry full identification with you at all times.
To open, break glass out.
If hammer breaks, replace immediately.
The line is busy.
Your battery's dead.
And, now, an important announcement from our sponsor.
I can't help you.
My skin itches.
Run, now, to your nearest dealer.
Walk, do not run, to the nearest exit.

I have lost my ticket.
Okay. Take off your clothes.
The pen of my aunt
the swimming pool of my uncle
leak.
Your dog just died.
You are dying.
Get ahead.
Think fast.
Don't worry.
Because of mechanical failure,
your insurance does not cover disaster.
Help me, Mr. No-One; I am drowning.
Death.

Your house is a parking lot now.
Aren't you drinking too much?
To call police, dial the operator.
If you need help, call, "Help!"
Now you take your statistics.
You write with a facility

which has held our attention.
Mama's plastic breast is deteriorating.
They all look alike to me.
Aren't you a member?

These are collectors' items.
Buy six and save.
One moment please . . .

The mountains look like Theodore Roosevelt.
Engineers who have graduated college
drain weedless lawns with concrete streambeds.
The birds are dying.
The tap water is full of liquid detergent.
The natives hate us.
I like everybody.
I said everybody.
Help me, Mr. No-One; I am drowning.
Well, that's life.
Death.
You can't fight progress.
It's not as attractive,
but the upkeep is less.
This is a friendly bank.
Ten years of continual expansion
and look at us now.
Not responsible.
Emergency only.
Offenders will be prosecuted
to the full extent of the law.
Out of order.
Please remit.
Your loved ones are preserved forever.
I didn't know it was loaded.
Watch your coat.
Honk your horn.
No passing.
No speeding.
Maintain speed.
Passengers are requested to remain seated.

Keep out. Keep off. Keep away.
Danger. Live wire.
Watch your step.
Mind your business.

I work with all-electric equipment.
My heart has a plastic pump.

My head revolves on a steel pin.
My parts are guaranteed.
Be prompt. Take your time !
Pay cashier. Pay when served.
Oh, before you go. When you get a chance.
You're tardy !—again.
The sun shines here an hour a day.
On Friday, at five, it rains.
The bottom rung
on the ladder of success
is temporarily broken.
Power is progress.
There will be a slight delay.
I'll never, ever take you out again.
We turned the switch, but nothing happened.
Stop crying.
You said you were coming yesterday.
This is the land of tomorrow.
Help me, Mr. No-One; I am drowning.
Death.

No ball-playing. No papers. No dogs.
Cover up; you're showing.
This, too, was once a wasteland.
It was your idea in the first place.
It's a piece of glass. It's a splinter.
It's a rusty nail and you're going to die.
Aren't you listening to what I'm saying?
You're odd, but you'll change.
—and you know it !
Get in line.
This park is for *your* enjoyment.

The policemen are here to help you.
Two dollars for indecent exposure.
Your round-trip ticket
is good for twenty-five years.
Prepare for war.
You brought the wrong papers.
The cranberries are malignant this year.
Water has pitted mother's stainless steel.
Plane trees resist carbon monoxide.
I really love the hurly-burly of the big city.

It's a fire engine; I thought it was an ambulance.
It figures. I'll check. I'll double-check.
You made a mistake.
You have been somewhat of a disappointment to us.
I want my penny back !
Push, don't pull.
Don't push !
Help me, Mr. No-One; I am drowning.
Death.

We're out of stock.
Help me, Mr. No-One: I am
Death.
They're all in storage.
Help me, Mr. No-One
Death.
They don't make this part any more.
Help me, Mr.
We can order one for you
Help me
Death.
If you didn't want it, why did you ask?
Help.
Death.
Okay !—sorry.
Help.
Death.

I said sorry.
Death.
Help.
Death.

Death.

Death.

The Land
(for Albizu Campos)

Our blue sea
now filled with cheap scum-bags
made in the USA
the continuous forests
now interrupted by coca-cola signs
the land something to buy
the yankee man touch everything
touch the sand
that saw Columbus
and our grass stepped on by Hush-Puppies
the Pueblo of my mother
of pretty music
of mid-night songs
now sold in stocks
the yankee hand
touching my land
the touch of hate
the touch of death
Albizu locked in a cell
spoke of new times to come
I freeze in New York
a native of a hot land.

And You Know It

And you know it
                    and you know it
and yes, you know it
and you know it as well as i do
    all there is to wisdom
                        we saw it all
        and we can tell everybody about it
        all there is to getting along with more than just getting
                                                    along
        to fighting our way thru all the lazy things
            that get in the way with getting along with
                you know we saw it
                a long time ago and haven't changed it
    yes you know all that

                        yes you do   you know it
            and we saw it all coming
        But didn't stop to change it
now all that has changed
            but we really do it
                and we know it
        too many comfortable things softened our backs
            and we knew it
            they were too easy
                        and we knew it
            before it all happend
                            we knew it
                            and didn't stop it
                                    no.

I Am a Multitude

In this life of unholy wars
man is now born with cranial puke and mucus
which spreads like the fire of a wheat field
in an open wind and settles
in prometheus rest on his tongue.

I am a pacifist.
Ordinarily I would not fight you.
But now that you challenge Phoebe,
who would better be forgotten,
and now that you stride to live with Ares,
I can not control the strain of my life
that has taught me to love.
I shall strike at your entrails
that are green with pungent rot.
With my very hands I shall abort the fungus
that was injected into you when you were born
and could hear.
This should first be rendered onto those
southern gentlemen
of refuted deliverance,
then spring to the infamous
northern enfolders
who have really taught us to hate.
God be willing, and I have ceased to question this,
and I can pull the knife from my breast
and mend my wounds,
Maybe someday I can forgive.
Standing on this threshold it is easy to sink deeper
into the muddy ebbless of stagnant ponds;
for all that I fight, I fight with;
yet it is Holy from unholiness.
All that I fight, I fight with as a weapon
because you are relative to the mind and
Holy when surfaced with love that will bore deep
into the core of your intrepid malady.

O Corpus Sanctum.
O Holy light, I call on you as Prometheus

to spark the smoldering embers of Phoenix.
This choice of resurrection is not for self;
for I am a multitude.

I, as we, in all of my ignorance,
am growing tired of flouncing in your corpulent sea
of human waste.
I, as we, stand ready now
to pull the nails from the fingers of any man
who raises the scythe.
I, as we, have heard too often the applause
from the magistrates of the Christian arenas.
I, as we, am tired of the building of pyramids.
I, as we, am tired of the oars of the gallows ship.
I, as we, am tired of the blade of the guillotine.
I, as we, am tired of the race to covet
the body-shells of other countries.
I, as we, am tired of the skeletal bodies
of living children.
I, as we, have felt the heat of too many ovens
of burning human flesh.
I, as we, have seen too long the stoical faces
of burning monks.
I, as we, have seen the deadly sleep of habit
on too many faces that walk in a trance.

And I, as myself, have seen enough of this cancer
on the face of humanity.

Goodbye Nkrumah

And yet, where would we be without the American Culture
Bye bye blackbird, as Miles plays it, in the '50's
Those coffee malteds?
When the radio told me there was dancing in the streets,
I knew we had engineered another coup;
Bought off another army.   And I wondered
what the boys at the Black Arts Theatre were saying
and sent them my love, and my prayers, which they would not
accept

Why should they?   it's their war, all I can do is wait
is not put detergents in the washingmachine, so the soil will
still be productive
when the black men, or the Chinese, come to cultivate it.

I remember a new photo of you stepping off a plane somewhere,
so cool, so straight a look, and so black.
There was nothing we could do but do you in.
You understand, of course.   There is nothing we can do

but shoot students
buy armies
like the British before us, killing the Zulus—
now they are fat and placid
their country a shambles.
Well, for us it won't end like that
not quite so simply
when the Nevele Country Club, the Hotel Americana
when Beverly Hills, and the Cliff House
come crashing down, it will be Shiva who dances,
the sky behind him orange (saffron) a great black mushroom
painted on it somewhere
(it was a mushroom killed Buddha)

will kill him again, compassion has to go

a few of us tried it, we tried to stop with printing
we tried to protect you with mimeograph machines

green poster LUMUMBA LIVES flooded Harlem in those
days
well, the best thing to do with a mimeograph is to drop it
from a five story window, on the head of a cop

we buy the arms and the armed men, we have placed them
on all the thrones of South America
we are burning the jungles, the beasts will rise up against us
even now those small jungle people with black eyes
look calmly at us out of their photographs
and it is their calm that will finish us, it is the calm
of the earth itself.

From Valley of Shadows

Moon cat, my nettle dancer
we will never make it to sun wheels;
to the changing shadows of reptiles.

Tonight, at crux
the winds blow,
high as grapes in Christ winter.
East on rawhide on whips,
on quivering islands:
black under plum, the winds blow.
From the straits of Messina,
full of mirage
and rain,

I miss you.

In actual hand comes summer
offer of Magi,
joined in our bodies.

When you touch me
we rise from bleached stone,

from dark water,
                    Fly away, demons !

Come home,
Love is at least a brown moth;
a seed pearl
born in the eye of the hangman.

Peyote Poem

I.

The way to God is
    anyway i walk; see; do;
i follow him to where
he hides, whenever time's too much
for him to buy off
    he sits and trembles,
    cooks up planets for his fix
                nods out on a skinny arm
    & dreams of
             potency, (his
    lost years balling Tibet and Africa
    before the loaves &
            lepers & rattle of
    politics cave in on him.
life's a chemical process so boorishly
prolonged you'd think that ornaments
or meat and bones had something
to do with
    purpose.
What glop to be remembered for!
he sighs, and his childish face glows again
    with a simpering lust.)

II.

i ignore my body just so long &
    forget where it ends
    (is that sea/that river/swamp
         is this machine
    my clumsy body?)
    Flapping on the shoals of instant
    like a ptarmigan
         plunging my beak into
    things concerning me
             no longer!
beliefs, possessions,
         attitudes;
    grotesque indelicate surrender
    to pressures of metabolism!
         and the will
    i forget where i used to
    think i ended and began.
i'm all sense and emptiness again,
    breathes me into form.

III.

it is vast and made of stars
it must be and is not.

Part IV: Book Allargando

        I have been
             a child
             in the world
                    while
the destinies of races
passed in exaggerated revue,
      the buffoons and sergeants
      of office and conviction
(cha cha cha !) obeying
      of occult
    and clownish tempos
(bomp bomp, boom boom boom).
         "Have you
seen the   bossa   nova?"
         "Have I
seen the   bossa   nova!"
        "Yeah, didn'
see the   bossa   nova?"
       ."Yes, I've
seen the   . bossa   nova!"
        If there is no one
        on the fence post
          you will
        look away.
One two three, one two three; one
                    two three,
          one
                two
                three.

                        Shimmy!
    If there is no one
    in the window
          you will
    reproduce.
And one and two, and three and four;
      and one and two,

and three and four.
This iron
is pitted,
this passing
is bitter.
Slow slow, quick quick slow;
slow slow,
tan -
go
close.

The Dead Man Dragged from the Sea

The dead man dragged from the sea
Lay on the beach on his heels, buttocks, shoulders.
Like the figure "X",
His arms and legs stretched outward, so the crowd,
Lunching on fingernails, had melted
Backward, there
Was nothing more that they could do.
On the quiet sea
A motorboat made disturbances.
This was the end of the sea . . .
What had he learned there?
Patience from the jellyfish?
        Had he learned the fruits of
Sensitive waiting, the turning
In wet seasons?—so the drift—
His mouth gaped wide, but someone had closed his eyes,
Denying all instruction
of the crystal mackerel.
"I live because I'm caught,
I fear and find no end to fear.
I never wanted to die,
Because I never thought of living."
And he came with a message from the anemones,
But though his tongue stared out
It never blinked—so then
The message of the squid
Was lost, and the revelations of the eels
Were lost,
And the warnings of the turtles—
For none could read
The darkening lips, the lids of salt.
        They were never sad enough
In burying the dead man dragged from the sea.

Pornography of Death
(To Florida)

honey, go out there
behind the tree
no one will see you, honey

There behind the tree
two green men
and a cart wait

For the stroke on the green
how clean youth must be
that's our job
one green man says to another

Honey, if you're not feeling well
go behind the tree and hide
there's a fine on talk of death

Honey, go behind the tree
and no one will see you, honey

There behind the tree
two green men
and a cart wait

If you can convince him
let him come quietly
we will shave him and
make him look eternal

Honey, there's a fine on death
I had a lunch of bouillon cubes
the radio said
we were the generation of
the youngest century

Honey, let them make you up
there's a fine on wrinkles

on sagging cheeks
the pinch test, honey,
have you passed it?

Pinch your stomach
your breast, your thigh
your neck, your skin
wherever it is
and then sing to the Senior
Youth is forever if you watch
out don't speak sadly, honey

Honey pay the fine
you said age
instead of Ponce de Leon
Go behind the tree there
the green is lighter
and on your stomach
you can rest forever
if they shave you first
if they dress you first
if they clean and perfume you
if they color your cheeks
if they convince me
you left successfully and
forever.

Barbara Gibson

After the Quarrel

After the quarrel
I melted
against his back, took
his hand hard in mine,
breathed
SOMEDAY WE'LL BE DEAD
and then oh baby we loved

Slap Happy

Doctor slaps
    Baby cries
Heck of a way to start life
    Lungs or no
Must air be that hard to come by
    Slapped to cry to breathe
Know what I did
    When the doctor's big hand
Whacked what little there was of me
    In his Hi boy meet the world
        I laughed
Gave his slap-me-down
        One big birth laugh
And I've been laughing
    Ski slopes of fun ever since
As long as there are people
        And power failures
    And transit strikes
        And taxes
    All whacking me
I'll laugh my birth laugh
        For very breath

Waters of my birth sac
        Broke to laughter
My laugh echoes canyons
    Explodes the glass
        Of my curtain wall office
I laugh the kisses of my plane bird
    Laugh traffic jams
        And standing lines
    And price rise
My birth stone is a laugh gem
    More facets than the tiffany diamond
I laugh the winds
        The sea waves
Laugh the sun to a gem on my finger

Poem for Adolph Eichman

Your lips pressed together
  Raising the left side
  of your face in a sneer
Remind me of the same
  Look of distraction you made
When my grandfather
  Presented you with butter
  in Vienna.
The price of his departure
  Was

         1 Farm - - - - - 160 Acres
         2 Tractors - - - New
         1 Building - - - Type-Lodge
         6 Laborers - - - Jewish

My grandfather
  Grumbled to his family later
That you had
  An uncultured taste
  Moved us from your presence.
In Argentina
  Where you both eventually
  Retreated to a café.

My grandfather
  Served you butter
And you recognized his face.
Later he sent a letter to me
Said: "I have seen my own
        Burning knife again.
        In the sloving butter
        The point appeared,
        Moved from my grasp

Stumbled into a pilot's arms
And was spirited away.
My grandson, like butter
We both have no feelings."
Now
How long can you hide
Your palpitations?
We know your sneer
Is a defense
You must know
Our butter knives
Are being sharpened.

Tune by Combo

Black eye like a sock
Stares down the sax
Poop-jay, and wow
Comes a sound to cry to.
Swollen bass fiddle
Pumps out miles of notes
For gazing at your greasy love.
Drink the jazz-glass,
Roll the jazz-glow in your gump;
Piano batters for you and that man
Gripping you across the table
With his aching eye.

Black, olive, silver white and flesh
Are the damned three

Throbbing in the dark
For gutter pay
And one watered whisky.

Mothers groaned and brought you out
To drape upon night's callous thumb;
Shoot out the stars
Bury silence with a glib roundelay
Of patent leather,
Knock down the trembling wall
Of sutured life that day makes better.
Hollow jerking on the small old chairs
May you pound in happiness
Or, if not,
Rout each tender thought
Till nothing's left but
     Tickle, mush, hush - eeedeeee.

Elvin Jones Gretch*—Freak
(Coltrane at the Half-Note)

To Elvin Jones/tub man of
 the John Coltrane Quartet.
(Gretch is the brand name of E.J.'s
drum set. GRETCH is outstanding on his
bass drum that faces the audience at
the Half-Note, Spring Street, New York City.)

gretch love
gretch hate
gretch mother   father fuck
fuck gretch
                    The Halfnote should be
                    a basement café like the "A" train
                    Jazz/drums of gretch
                    on the fastest and least stopping
                    transportation scene in NYC
                    subways are for gretch
                    "A" train long as a long city block
                    the tenements of the underground rails
                    West 4th
                    34th   42nd   125th
            farther down in the reverse
                              local at west 4th
        waterfront   warehouse   truck/produce   vacant
        the halfnote
                    our city fathers keep us on the right track
zones/   ozone
                    fumes of tracks   /smokestacks
                    Con Edison billows cinders   soot
                    over the UN   East River   14th Street
                    on the East side
The Halfnote
westside truck exhaust and spent breath
of Holland Tunnel   exhaust   soot darkness jazz
speeding cars   noisy/   noiseless
speeding gretch   tremulous gretch

Elvin Jones the man behind the pussy
four men love on a stage
the loud orgy
gretch trembles and titters
                    gretch is love
                    gretch is love
                    gretch is love

Elvin's drum ensemble the aggressive cunt
the feminine mystique
cymbals tinny clitoris   resounding
lips snares flanked/   encircling
thumping foot drum peter rabbit the fuck   take
this   and take   that
elvin behind the uterus of his sticks
the mad embryo
panting sweat-dripping embryo
misshapen/   hunched
Coltrane sane/   cock   the forceps
the fox and the   hare
the chase
screaming and thumping
traffic of music on Spring Street
'Trane   says to young apprentice Ron Feral   "Fill in the
    solids;
get it while it's hot and comely;   Elvin fucks almost as
    good as his Mama."

The Halfnote is as packed as   rush hour on 42nd & 8th
"A" train territory
coltrane is off with a hoot
directed supine
nowhere in generalness
into the din and the death
between   bar and tables   reds silver glass molten mass shout
tobacco fumes across the boardwalk
                    (coney island is the "D" train change
                    at west 4th if you want it)
Coltrane steps the catwalk
                    elvin jones drums gretch
                    gretch shimmy and shout
elvin drums a 1939 ford

99 pushing miles per hour/   shoving barefoot driver
                         in the heats
Coltrane/Jones
riffing   face to face
instruments charge
        stools to kneecap
many faceted rhythm structure   to tomahawk
gretch rocks   'n rolls   gretch rattles
fuck gretch/
                we know so well strident drums
                children singing death songs/war
                tenor   and soprano   high
tenor soar/   flux of drums chasing
                inviolate   blue
the model "T" ford & air hammer
                Holland tunnel
                Avenue of the Americas
                cobbled stones/   din   of rubber
                of tin
to the truck graveyard
line-up of Boston Blackie nights/   deserted
right here model "T" & tomahawk
                sometimes late in silent din of night
                I hear
                bagpipes/   death march
                    music of ago/   kennedy
gretch gretch tune optical color-jumping gretch
            Elvin's F-86 Sabre jet/   remember Korea/
                Horace Silver
            the fine smooth jackets the colored boys brought
                back
            from the far east with "U.S. Air Force" (or whatever)
                blazing the back   —a forgotten flame

Elvin tom-tomming
bassing the chest "E"/gretch   "J"/gretch
                clashing metal mad
                tin frantic road of roaring/   gretch
                roar
peck morrison
the *bass* player
told me once about a drum set

with a central anchor/   every drum connected

        unable to jump or sway
        drums like the cockpit of a TXF spy plane
        ejaculator seat and all
                (call up brubecks joe dodge, al hirt
                Lester Lanin et al)
Pilot conflict
and the man elvin behind the baptismal tubs
that leap like cannons   to the slashing sound   of knives
black elvin knows so well
the knives the Daily News displays along with the photo
of a grinning award-winning cop
the kind of knives elvin talks about
downtown by the water
and uptown
near the park

Jitterbugging in the Streets
(To Ishmael Reed)

There will be no holy man crying out this year
No seer, no trumpeter, no George Fox walking barefeet
          up and down the hot land
The only messiah we shall see this year
Staggers
To and fro
On the LowerEastSide
Being laughed at by housewives in Edsel automobiles
          who teach their daughters the fun of deriding a
          terror belched up from the scatological asphalt
          of America
Talking to himself

An unshaven idiot
A senile derelict
A black nigger
Laughter and scorn on the lips of Edsel automobiles
     instructing the populace to love God, be kind to
          puppies
              and the Chase Manhattan National Bank

Because of this there will be no Fourth-of-July this year
No shouting, no popping of firecrackers, no celebrating,
          no parade
But the rage of a hopeless people
Jitterbugging
in
the streets

Jacksonville Florida
Birmingham, Atlanta, Rochester, Bedford
Stuyvesant, Jersey City, Chicago,
Jackson Mississippi, Harlem New York—
Watts L.A.
Jitterbugging
          in
          the streets
To ten thousand rounds of ammunition
To water hoses, electric prods, phallic sticks,

hound dogs, black boots stepping in soft
places of the body—
Venom is in the mouth of Christian housewives,
smart young Italians, old Scandinavians in
Yorkville, suntanned suburban organization
men, clerks and construction workers, poor
white trash and gunhappy cops everywhere
"Why don't we kill all the niggers.
Not one or two
But every damn black of them.   Niggers will do
anything.
I better never catch a nigger messing with my wife,
And most of all never with my daughter !   Aughter
grab 'em up and ship every black clean out of
the country . . . Aughter just line 'em up and
mow 'em down
Machine Gun Fire!"
Mississippi
Georgia
Tennessee, Alabama
Your mother your father your brothers, sisters, wives
and daughters
Up and down the hot land
There is a specter haunting America
Spitfire of clubs, pistols, shotguns, and the missing
Mutilated
Murdered
Bodies of relatives and loved ones
Be the only Santa Claus niggers will remember this year
Be the only Jesus Christ born this year
curled out dead on the pavement, torso floating
the bottom of a lake
Being laughed at by housewives in Edsel automobiles
You say there are four gates to the ghetto
Make your own bed hard that is where you have got
To lay
You say there is violence in Harlem, niggers run amuck
perpetrating crimes against property, looting
stores,
breaking windows, flinging beer bottles at officers
of the law

You say a certain virgin gave birth to a baby
Through some mysterious process, some divine conjure—
A messenger turned his walking cane into a serpent
        and the serpent stood up and walked like a natural
man;
You say . . . .

America, why are you afraid of the phallus !

I say there is no violence in Harlem.
There is TERROR in Harlem !
And Fear !   And corruption !   And murder !
Harlem is the asphalt plantation of America
Rat infested tenements totter like shanty houses
        stacked upon one another
Circular plaque of the welfare check brings vicious wine
        every semi-month, wretched babies twice a year,
death
All Americans. Housewives, businessmen, civil
service employees, loving their families, going to
church regularly depositing money in their
neighborhood bank,
All Fourth-of-July celebrators belched up from
        the guilt-ridden cockroach, sick sex terror
        of America
Talking to themselves
in bars
On street corners,
Fantasizing hatred
At bridge clubs
Lodge meetings, on park benches,
in fashionable mid-town restaurants—

No Holy man shall cry out upon the black ghetto this year
No trombonist
The only messiah we will know this year is a bullet
in the belly
of a Harlem youth shot down by a coward crouched
        behind an outlaw's badge—

        and hopelessness every time the sun goes down
Big bellied agents of down-town landlords forcing black girls

to get down and do the dog before they learn to
spell
their names
If you make your bed hard
He said he was fifteen years old, and he walked beside us
there in the littered fields of the ghetto
He spoke with a dignity of the language that shocked us
and he said he had a *theory* about what *perpe-
trated* the
Horror that was upon us as we walked among flying bullets,
broken glass, curses and the inorganic phalluses of
cops
whirling about our heads
He said he was a business major at George Washington High
And he picked up a bottle and hurled it above the undulating
crowd
Straight into the chalk face of a black helmet—

Thirty seven properties ransacked, steel gates ripped from
their hinges, front panes shattered, pawn shops,
dry
cleaners, liquor stores
Ripped apart and looted—
Niggers will do anything !
And if your church don't support the present
Police Action,
In dingy fish-n-chip and bar-b-que joints
The niggers will go on doing business as usual—
From river to river,
Signboard to signboard
Scattering Schaefer six-packs all over the ghetto,
Like a bat out of hell,
Marques Haynes is a dribbling fool
TERROR is in Harlem
A GENOCIDE so blatant
Every third child will do the junky-nod in the whore scented
night before semen leaps from his loins
A FEAR so constant
Black men crawl the pavement as if they were snakes,
and snakes turn to sticks that beat the heads of
those
who try to stand up—

And Fourth-of-July comes with the blasting bullet in the belly
   of a teenager
Against which no Holy man, no Christian housewife
n Edsel automobile
Will cry out this year
   Jitterbugging
     in
     the streets!

In Moloch's Eye
(In memory of three young men murdered
near Philadelphia, Mississippi.)

You bruised your feet, grape dark on spear heads.
Scar tissue sandals them upon the road
welled in by brambles crackled to vituperation,
and by trees, sky fountain shot, leaping,
their lancet leaves snapped off in volleys,
in single curses, broken against your shields.

Shadrach, your wounds are moist upon the ash.
Winds shall no longer stop our lungs
with dust of anger shaken from fallacies.
Meschach, your feet have burned
poison from cinders. No longer shall they fall upon our heads,
eating the bone away, corrosive
in labyrinths of brain.

Meirut, Abednego, in seeded hearth,
dance all the nodes of danger to Perseids,
freed at maturity of summer, souls
leaving a legend for an instant on the sky
before returning to the darkness
where they germinate beneath the edge of earth
and rise as stars.

Behind your roaring curtain we have seen you pass,
enter and exit on rhythms of history.
Beside, in front of, and behind you there is One,
now melting into many, now individual,
now man who turns to beast, turns eagle, bull or lion, moves,
stands motionless beyond all forms within the nullifying
writhing and twisting essence of the fire.

How many times must you return?   Upon
what blossomed antler of the universe
must you again appear, fire walkers, marching barefoot

through a reek that blinds a generation which only hears
sackbut and psaltery, which fails to follow feet
printing a signature exultant upon the coals,
dancing vainglory into clinkers, bounding,
passionate within destruction, fire kernel freezing
greed at is fountainhead beneath the flames?

Kauri

Kauri is a Hindi word for the cowry shell, that
spiral of implicit coil, of smooth natural porcelain ex-
terior, of vagina-toothed under, inscending into infinite
inwards on those vibrations of our inmost reach, opening
outward again in the same, as the spiral Self, opening
and opening, suddenly realizes I Never WAS NOT Center but
forever and forever AM in perfect and indivisible inter-
course with all of mySelf in all of yourSelf . . . perfect
and indivisible, yes, yet not without the anguish of ebb,
the shredding of tidal withdrawal, the sharp thrust of
encounter and aggress, the terrible imposition of unready
necessities in rhythms we must outreach and transcend
with that AM, that perpetual Wholeness even in our frag-
ment selves . . .

KAURI never justifies but ever seeks to understand, and, where understanding fails, to experience,
deeper than ego and light and mind, that terrible and
mysterious inner Darkness, that seeming Abyss, without
which our harmony is petty and trivial, without which
our love is a mockery and our victory a shallow death.
Bring your opposites here, not to *me,* but to you in me,
to me in you, that, where we were separate and opposite,
we, remaining individual and sacred, are violable and broken
upon the Wholeness which, o Blessed Tygers and Lambs, we
perpetually and fierce joyfully ARE!

Marvin Jackman

Blues for Lucifer

No tomorrow for him,
He stole yesterday
  from me
Put all my yesterdays
  in his pocket
Ain't that cold, man?
Thought I would be there
  Always . . . kissing.
Call me tomorrow:
  FU 1-9650
His shit stinks
But the klan burned
  my outhouse
Ain't that cold, man?
Wait 'til the shit
  hits the fan
When his yesterday
  is dust
When he's choked
  on the bitter-
  sweetness of life
When the motherfuckin
  sun sets in the west
  of his heart
Won't that be cold, man . . .

Poem to Americans

I watched the road - as the white boys play:
Then as a bush - Then as a cloud passing over
I dig his arrogant wartime -
                                    marching up and down
The sunlight deepened into the trees   tympani heralded
- dust went puff puff like fat men rejects
                          of the Third Reich
Behind hob nails flashing, fascinated Jew smiling
While the white boys play

-Then as a drum, Then flags rolling on the wind
They came with the hand jive - Cry, crying goodbye
as the sky dims and new day - was a white boy

So this was the Teutonic experience alas I know him well
All his toys are stamped mine -
Down the road the farmer grins - the house mother gleaming -
the sound and dreaming triumph strike the brain cell spit,
And the pussy is wet -
Wet with cells and whips of sweating burning drinking death -
And lost thighs stand back to back
Still they ate and laid on the sweet scent -
carried on carried on carried on the white boy
-Grabbed my dick: Your name is dick he said
                          You cannot stay he said
Then swift I did a sex dance before his eyes
The dance was gone - march - whirling and whirling
As the white boys play.

Up and down the road where dust clouds rise
stayed all night pounding pounding for life -
and dividends

If I Ride This Train

If I ride this train
The long lean road
The weary road with specks of blood that punctuate
Your movement of poverty
The road of fat asses singing joyous hymns to
Life, to love, to lime, to ash
Cracked souls of pimps weep beneath the junkies jagged heel
In the night of the beginning excerpts of blood bless
The feet of the unloved
And if I ride this train when the deal goes down
The baby's pablum eyes will awake with the laughter of
Crocodiles
When the deal goes down and if I ride this train
On my nigger streets warm with neglect flowers will bloom
To greet cement pigeons
Harsh rhythms will repeat themselves to the ear of a blind
Man: Nigger boy, Nigger Man
                         Liv'in hard—Live if can!
If I ride this train I want a hotline to Jesus
I want to dance and draw blood
I want to grin and speak serpents
I want
I wanta' hiss love through my intervenous jungle
Through the trash crowded eye of my quick-soon street
In a full-lipped song
To a junkman
Cut
Cut with a razor
Bleeding tears
When the deal goes down
Black women in Hallelujah white singing blood

                                        soaked shouts
To Daddy Grace and Father "D"
And if I ride this pain
Pain will transduce this train
If I ride this train
Beyond theocratic reservations
My address will be unknown except to god and the
Boogaman.

Canto #4

I Bos Taurus spatha,
Spading the pinto bean earth
Like a wintergreen rubbed down
Sprinter before the gun,
Have repulsed the picadores
Under the E-flat trumpet-sun.

And banderillas that burn
Like angry chili peppers
Sprout-from my casserole shoulders
Like a Navajo ruler's headdress.

And already my C-natural blood
Is seeping like liquid roses.

And my ears dance to the music
From the translucent chorus.

And your suit-of-lights, more
Translucent than the chorus,
Radiates its rainbow energy
On a shrill brass ascent.

So whirl your cape-baby !

From First They Slaughtered the Angels

I.

First they slaughtered the angels
tying their thin white legs with wire cords
and
opening their silk throats with icy knives
They died fluttering their wings like chickens
and their immortal blood wet the burning earth

we watched from underground
from the gravestones, the crypts
chewing our bony fingers
and
shivering in our piss stained winding sheets
The seraphs and the cherubim are gone
they have eaten them and cracked their bones for marrow
they have wiped their asses on angel feathers
and now they walk the rubbled streets with
eyes like fire pits

II.

who finked on the angels?
who stole the holy grail and hocked it for a jug of wine?
who fucked up Gabriel's golden horn?
   was it an inside job?

who barbecued the lamb of god?
who flushed St. Peter's keys down the mouth of a
North Beach toilet?
who raped St. Mary with a plastic dildo stamped with the
Good Housekeeping seal of approval?
                        was it an outside job?

where are our weapons?
where are our bludgeons, our flame throwers, our poison
gas, our hand grenades?
we fumbled for our guns and our knees sprout credit cards,
we vomit canceled checks

standing spreadlegged with open sphincters weeping soap suds
from our radioactive eyes
and screaming
for the ultimate rifle
the messianic cannon
the paschal bomb

the bellies of women split open and children rip their
way out with bayonets
spitting blood in the eyes of blind midwives
before impaling themselves on their own swords

the penises of men are become blue steel machine guns,
they ejaculate bullets, they spread death as an orgasm

lovers roll in the bushes tearing at each other's genitals
with iron finger nails

fresh blood is served at health food bars in germ free
paper cups
gulped down by syphilitic club women
in papier maché masks
each one the same hand-painted face of Hamlet's mother
at the age of ten

we watch from underground our eyes like periscopes
flinging our fingers to the dogs for candy bars
in an effort to still their barking
in an effort to keep the peace
in an effort to make friends and influence people

III.

we have collapsed our collapsible bomb shelters
we have folded our folding life rafts
and at the count of twelve
they have all disintegrated into piles of rat shit
nourishing the growth of poison flowers
and venus pitcher plants
we huddle underground
hugging our porous chests with mildewed arms
listening to the slow blood drip from our severed veins

lifting the tops of our zippered skulls
to ventilate our brains
          they have murdered our angels

we have sold our bodies and our hours to the curious
we have paid off our childhood in dishwashers and miltown
and rubbed salt upon our bleeding nerves
in the course of searching
          and they have shit upon the open mouth of god
they have hung the saints in strait jackets and they have
tranquilized the prophets
they have denied both christ and cock
and diagnosed buddha as catatonic
emasculated the priests and the holy men and
censored even the words of love
          Lobotomy for every man!
and they have nominated a eunuch for president
          Lobotomy for the housewife!
          Lobotomy for the business man!
Lobotomy for the nursery schools!
and they have murdered the angels

IV.

now in the alleyways the androgynes gather swinging their
lepers' bells like censers as they prepare the ritual
rape of god

          the grease that shines their lips is the
fat of angels
          the blood that cakes their claws is the
blood of angels

they are gathering in the streets and playing dice with
angel eyes
they are casting the last lots of armaggedon

V.

now in the aftermath of morning
we are rolling away the stones from underground, from the
caves
we have widened our peyote-visioned eyes
and rinsed our mouths with last night's wine

we have caulked the holes in our arms with dust and flung
libations at each other's feet

and we shall enter into the streets and walk among them and
do battle
holding our lean and empty hands upraised
we shall pass among the strangers of the world like a
bitter wind
and our blood will melt iron
and our breath will melt steel
we shall stare face to face with naked eyes
and our tears will make earthquakes
and our wailing will cause mountains to rise and the sun to
          halt

THEY SHALL MURDER NO MORE ANGELS!

          not even us

Poems from Oklahoma

. . . Who is Bernice
that savage impulse I go to
on my 3 day pass to town?
She drinks.   She farts.
She loves me.
We carouse in bars,
drink away her flesh
and her 3 weird sisters
Topsy, Flossie and Gina;
they sew a garment for us.
One weaves.   One unravels.
One cuts.

                         Who is Bernice
wild indian of Lawton I
love?   When I'm away
she waits in bars
exclaiming in her drink
"I love that big jew."
When she left me
after a month
I went wild.
All the sergeant said -
that Apache Dido
waits for all men.
She's been pregnant 3 months.
Oh, who is Bernice?
If I stuck my arm up
to the elbow
there would only be the wind.

Benediction

Pale brown Moses went down to Egypt land
To let somebody's people go.
Keep him out of Florida, no UN there:
The poor governor is all alone,
With six hundred thousand illiterates.

America, I forgive you . . . I forgive you
Nailing black Jesus to an imported cross
Every six weeks in Dawson, Georgia.
America, I forgive you . . . I forgive you
Eating black children, I know your hunger.
America, I forgive you . . . I forgive you
Burning Japanese babies defensively—
I realize how necessary it was.
Your ancestor had beautiful thoughts in his brain.
His descendants are experts in real estate.
Your generals have mushrooming visions
Every day your people get more and more
Cars, televisions, sickness, death dreams.
Your must have been great
Alive.

Millennium

They have lined you against a wall, God
They have forced you to dig a bottomless pit, God
They have raped your wives, God
They have taken your son and beat his head against a brick
post, God
They have pulled out your fingernails, God
They have applied electrodes to your penis, God
And to the nipples of your mother
Where the pain is more than pain, God
They have ravished your daughter, God
They have dragged your grandfather by his beard through
the streets
of Polish Russian/Czechoslovakian/Lithuanian/Hungarian/
Italian/German/Latvian/Bulgarian/Serbian/Yugoslavian
towns, God
They have burned your Grandmother's hair, God
They have buried your books of the law, God
They have killed, God
They have killed you, God

Flower Passion

I want to fuck flowers
Flowers want to suck me
Kinsey should have given me a chapter
I would go down in fucken history.

Daffodils and tiger lilies
open up their fleshly lips
I would dare the thorns of horror
For a taste of red rose hips.

You may keep your birds and wild bees
You may keep your soft does eyes
Nor can sweetgirls passion equal
Sweet peas coming through the rye.

Autumn 1964

        Sitting here in the night with
darkness heaped in every corner,
wondering if you can read my writing,
because that's the only light I have.
The morning's coming. I can hear the
garbage trucks singing like city
crickets, collecting the night.
Thinking that of the new songwriters,
I'm the oldest and the most evil with
my past. I have no lies to tell
about my past and sometimes it
strangles me like a black dog putting
his foot down my throat. I am not so
wild as I was once; I'm pretty good
about it. I haven't gotten the rabies
of shadow in my teeth except once or
twice in the last six months. I
always rage most at those I love,
and mostly for good reasons. And to
those to whom I did, my apologies.
But you may have deserved it.

        Someone once said to me "I envy
you your heart, but I couldn't stand
your hangovers." And oh, how I have
fallen for you, you high-stepping,
wrap-around chrome-popsickle girls.
For the right pair of legs, and God save us from
the probable barbed wire of blonde hair. And
I'll do it well, and if there are few men that
do that any more they get oriented to be sane
too soon. And it's because I am mad and can't
help it.

        I always love like a high jack-rabbit going
through a bramble. Or a hawk up there twining the
world around him just before he falls to get the
jack, like an eight-wheeler going through a Kansas
town at midnight, with only a little boy watching

from his bedroom window and riding every non-stop
car out. I love like an act of nature.

Not casual, my love.
But like a tender trumpet.
Softly.
Proudly.
Loudly.
Lostly.
In the thunderheads my dark,
My love.
Not casual . . .

O the Beatniks Never Win and
They Done the Poets in and They Hangin
All the Beatles in the Mornin

In the Interest of Public Decency,
the Defenders of Our Rights,

the Dispensers of Our Justices,
the Quagmires of All that's Good and True
                in America—
(I'm talking bout the cops, in case you don't
recognize anybody you know in there)
went around real quiet-like
and closed the poem-readings
over there in Greenwich Village

Talkin about: Every Liter-ary Bit Hurts, y'know?

Because of a lack of Private Funds
(it rained a lot that year, and
the Payola crop was late)
 the previously-mentioned Defenders, Dispensers,
              and Quagmires
righteously closed the murky dens
where Free Love, Intermarriage, and Peace
were discussed aloud,
where iambics were furtively passed
from hand to hand
beneath the tables,
where a stick of pure Ginsberg
brought a dollar-ninety-five tops,
and where us poets worked
our excess egos off
on each others' crippled ear.

Looks Like: A Cleaner New York Is Up To The Screws.

Of course, we didn't take it sitting down.
Somebody organized a Cappuchino Orgy,
and we met in Union Square
and recklessly swilled cups of it

in the face of a Maddened Populace.
The cops just yawned
and things broke up
when we ran out of whipped cream.

Then we wrote three-hundred-forty-seven poems,
protesting all this stuff,
and all but ninety-four were published
Several middle-classed and forward-thinking folks
objected,
and the New York Daily News
even ran an editorial.
About something.
For a change.
So to capitalize on the publicity
Schrafft's announced
a poem-reading.
The Culture-Starved thronged in,
and it was a great success;
the white-shirt-and-tied young poets,
cleanly shaven, read their sonnets.
(One, called "God Walks in My Garden,"
even brought a thunderous polite response.)

Nedick's, Woolworths,
the Chase Manhattan Bank,
and White Rose Bars
all quickly followed suit,
and America became, again,
a Citadel of Culture,
a rumbling fount of rhyme and meter,
sweeter by far
than the Graveyard gloomy days
when poets had had something
to rebel about.

Maury Fishbein brought about a Renaissance.
Do not forget that, friends.
Maury Fishbein died
that other poets might live,

and forever draw into their lungs
the clean, clear air of Freedom.

It is to him, his memory
to which I dedicate
these humble lines.

in the little magazines,
and three were finally anthologized
to the Everlasting Credit
of The Movement.

Summer came.   The Village streets, deserted.
(Except for the fairies, finks, rough trade,
junkies, jerk-offs, pushers, tourists, folk-
singers, and people waiting for the 8th Street
Crosstown bus.)

It looked like poetry was dead.
But, as almost always in the history
of Homo Sap.,
a leader rose in our most darkest hour.
Of all the paradoxes that we've seen
in this bright earth,
I think that Maury Fishbein was
the most:

he was a poet
and
he was a man.

On Labor Day, he took a match,
a marijuana cigarette,
and three quarts of gasoline
to the very steps of City Hall.
Invocating verses from
The Gospel According to Lawrence Ferlinghetti,
he doused himself with gas,
lit up, drew one deep breath,
and plunged the stick of pot into his belly.

What was left of him was then arrested
for creating a public nuisance,

disturbing the police,
and burning trash between the hours
of nine and five.

He got his picture in Life magazine,
and there was lots of talk.

From In the Time of Revolution

IV.

One needs a lyric poet in these
now nights (dawns)
at 27 because revolution
is not
banners unfurling on clear
afternoons,
nor songs
(We Shall Overcome our own
inadequacies Someday,
O Lord.
Have mercy upon us.
Have Mercy upon us.)
heard in the distance.
the heartbeat of
revolution is
women
(in China and Algeria maybe it was different)
knowing that
(yes)
it must be
but in their
woman
(women)
souls
needing to ask him
(who lives only in now)
"do you think she needs a sweater today?"   "Do you
think she has a temperature?" "What's good on t.v. tonight?"
the minutiae of the day
un-
ra-
vels
(in the same way each day because God
rewinds the yarn each night and puts the neatly
wound ball back in your sewing basket each dawn)
and to keep from being
choked in its threads
the woman
(blood in the veins of poets)
needs someone to hold out their

(him)
un-
winds
because
night is
heavy
and as she lies down
it is like a
tombstone and her
bed a
grave dug by him in his
dawn
dawn
dawning of
now.

V.

It cannot be
reasoned with,
revolution,
nor even
understood.
It can only be
endured.   (like labor.   Will there
ever be a Lamaze of revolution?)
Not for ideals, commitments
or any of those things
we thought
(at night, before the dawn with tea
and cigarettes and many books).
Revolution is.

VI.

One needs a lyric poet in this
now
dawn (nights)
because he lives like the
hawk knowing that
what has been
will always be
and as we
(even he, too)
nail ourselves to
crosses he must be there,
pinioned,
because

atlanta, georgia
november 20, 1966

D. A. Levy

Ode to Mayor Locker
(R. E. vision for Phil Ochs)

     Home Is the Hunky

the dogs are in uniforms at the Hough Ave airport
waiting to greet you & the people with dog minds
the people in dog suits - the dog mind   a
       HA HA   you old rascal
you're not a police dog - you're in drag
I see yr zipper   ole mayor locker/
unzip old ralphy & we got   "GOTT IN HIMMEL"
In Super Service the gasstation mechanic - the
       Pharoah of Fairview Park

The maniac Buddha mind of Brookpark Village
is an ibis/ a swallow/ a phoenix/
       its SUPER funk,
you ain't even a bad guy
               you're like prez johnson
               who plays
               strange new forms of music
               "jazz politics"
                  "Fug the people" (it seems ive

heard that riff before
Ole Magyar of Swamp Erie - your empty face
             you aint even a bad guy
             you are just one of the replaceable
             3 Stooges
             Ralph/ Larry & Moe

Ole wise man of Cleveland
you're just like prez johnson
who plays
musical electric chairs
With The People
   & the parades of parades
   & uniforms of death all look the same to me
Ole Magyar/ the hungarians died for freedom 1956
& you are selling ours with your blank face in 1966

Ole Mayor Locker
     you aint even smart enough to be a bad guy
     & the parades of parades of death
     whisper in the marching   marching
     of the   4th Reich . . .

                              America

We Were All There Together, Really

We were all there:
>   waving at the TV camera
>   playing Monopoly
>   shoes off in the Vista dome
>   sleeping in the Scenicruiser
>   eating blintzes in Phoenix
>   Pastrami in Yokohama
>   getting three tunes for a quarter
>   everywhere.

We were all there, together, really:
>   When Bob Seider pulled out the jukebox cord
>   in West Kansas
>   and played How High the Moon for the people
>   on his tenor:
>   when Sleepy in Japan played New Orleans blues;
>   when Ivan in Hongkong played New York bebop;
>
>   when Joe in the blackout in Carlsbad Cavern
>   played his flute,
>   in bat guano
>   constant 56 degree temperature

We were all there:
>   when Buddy sat in the Orgone box and had a fix;
>   when Sam rolled up his sleeve in the Chicago
Hotel
>   that morning and got hooked
>   (and it wasn't what he got hooked on
>   that killed him, it was
>   what he knew, he said.)

All there:

>   under the skylight
>   whistling Debussy
>   smoking Dr. R. Schiffman Asthmador Jimson
Weed Cigarets.

And we were all there:

When they invented
        Mum
        Void
        Fab
        Ajax
        Zonite
        Cherry-flavored spermicidal jelly
        4 minute mile
        plastic reeds
        the ether kick

We were all there
        when Life magazine made mushrooms.

We were all there,
        buying swamp shiners
        high laughter
        Sophoclean
        bruxating
        digging the fireworks at Pontchartrain Beach
        digging the man on the swaying high-pole
        digging the fan belts that looked like snakes
        (and the snakes that looked like fan belts)
        listening to the bells in Santa Fe
        calling the living
        lamenting the dead . . .

We were all there:

        when D. H. Lawrence was on tympani
        Tom Wolfe on Steinway
        Walt Whitman and Sherwood Anderson on Tenor
        God on bass:
        Charts by Jesus, Buddy Bolden
        everybody using the same ashtray . . .

We were all there:
        waving back at the hillside Picasso men
        who turned out to be Saguaro cactuses
        keeping right except to pass

watching the curves
staying alert
watching for slow trucks
fast rocks
caught in the cattle guard
parked on the median
handcuffed on the freeway
not seeing the Berkeley Railroad sign
"stop when swinging."

We were all there together, really.
Still, now, always, rotating, revolving,
dancing,
now,
always,
together.

Safari

COME with me
on a safari
into the teeming
jungle darkness
of a black soul
searching for
itself

trek with me
thru these vast
congos

arkansas alabama
mississippi
can you follow me

DEALER
SIGN in a
mississippi
junkyard

we
buy
burnt
bodies

The Result Is Not Zero
(A found poem from a letter by Frederick Engels)

History makes itself in such a way
        that the final result always arises
from conflicts between many individual wills
        of which each again has been made what it is
by a host of particular conditions of life.
        Thus there are innumerable intersecting forces
an infinite series of parallelograms of forces
        which give rise to one resultant—
                the historical event.
This again may be viewed
        as the product of a power
which taken as a whole
        works *unconsciously* and without volition.
For what each individual wills
        is obstructed by everyone else
and what emerges is something
                that no one willed.
Thus past history proceeds
        in the manner of a natural process
and is also essentially subject
        to the same laws of movement.
But from the fact that individual wills—
        of which each desires
what he is impelled to
        by his physical constitution
and external, in the last resort
        economic circumstances (either his own
personal circumstances or those
        of society in general)—
do not attain what they want
        but are merged into a collective mean
a common resultant
        it must not be concluded
that their value $= 0$.
        On the contrary
each contributes
        to the resultant
and is to this degree
        involved in it.

American Setup

I.

Irish cop, a smile a day, on corner:
            "it's a great life, a great life."
While wops/ Jews/ dagoes/ niggers
USA-their-way jobward:
city scene comes breezing in. The scatterbrain
America's Song, this—finally. "great life . . .
                  if you don't weaken." If. But. And
                              if but and.
Beefy cop with jaws of the bulldog; worm
hands hustle the cowboy who sleeps with sissies
in L.A.—in N.Y. Cowboy: "now listen here, hear!"
now YOU just listen."
                  cowboy: "up your bloody cunt cop!"
                  "Yeah he's an American citizen,
                  just like you—burning his bridges
                  behind him." Scatterbrain. If—but . . .
Foul bum, fifty years of German & English stock
tattered coat, wine bottle, old penis diseased
hanging between the hooks. Says: "run to the mill,
run to the mill,"
out of a clear blue sky, breaks his wine bottle
                  in honor of the Church.

II.

On the El train, Negro girl: "Girl, I wipe
      their ole pink asses, I'm sick." "You still
            an aid in dat hospital, chile?" The city
comes clean with me.
A dime a dozen, the scatter   the scatter brain.
The bum in the subway peeing on the post:
comes clean with me.
The Irish cop swinging his billie against the heads
            of Harlem/ South Side. Scream: "Come clean
with me." But that's all she rotes.
"it's a great life if you don't weaken/ come clean."
Sissy says: "they dragged me into court."
The walls fall. The speed of the cars on the city;

the level, the break/ "these people
                    crazy as a bedbug."   & all fools.
Cob webs hang on cowboy as he tries to switch
                    over to: a stripper—She makes it.
Big. Hips, and lips: say, she says: "You come
                    breezing in here, and think."
"Well I got news for you," says sister.
Red lips, green eyes, yellow hair, fade out.
Naked except. "All I hear, see is dicks, cunts
        pussies, asses, and horny old men."
& cowboy is sick of her already. On the stairway:
"Lets tear off a quickie."

III.

Once she knew a babyfaced blue eyed Bank President.
Ounces of sperm, from him. "An apple a day keeps the
                                doctor away." But
        he was Nothing. All figures/ money.
The smallest "thing" "I ever saw, girlie: & when
                        it stood up, it
                        was no bigger than
                        my little finger. See?"
Negro nurse's aid, on corner of Irish ownership:
her pimp, breezing, leaning back into shadows
where stripper & cowboy fled: "I kicked it babe/
                    I kicked the habit;
                    honest to god, I used
                        & it was nice. Now:
I kicked." "Well don't get hooked no more Joe."
No Jonas tip played on me, sugar whispers a secret
                    dream.Dream of jeanie with the
        light brown bag
of goodies.   "I used and it was boss. I tell you boss."
The sissy comes. "Say honey did you dig Jack Benny
last night joking about?" A Lincoln dollar in my hand;
a 'Vashington coin; a Jefferson transcript—streets
named these names. Deep American history of pain:
Nat Turner on horseback with flames in hand, riding
to heaven. Malcolm X on the cross.
Ben Casey stroking a brown girl's shoulder.

IV.

Grandma pants as she hangs clothes on the
      American clothes line. Indiscreet wife of the
      eternal general, listens to her washing machine
                  hum. The refrigerator door
of junior's jam dreams slams on puppies nose.
Over-alls wearing nobodies in good health
                  go forth, to punch time cards
and IBM work cards/ each oblong hole has
      a meaning. "A fool's gold. You ever
wuz able to buy a new car Charlie? Me neither."
"Dat Norma Jean Monroe gal sure was a beautiful
                  sad girl wasn't she?"
Ernest Hemingway did the same thing.
Robert Williams *is* the black man in exile—
                  China, Cuba. No sad Billie Holiday
                  song upon his pulse.
A robin hood of the century, hung on the cross
            to rot. Flies buzzing in the casements.
Mahalia Jackson does the funeral of the Irish cop,
with an ever growing sadness. Charlie Chinaman (USA)
            catches his victim. "Bubble gum kid,
on the loose." Spinning top johnny, balloon jacks, etc.
In short: the gashouse kids, Brooklyn smith, etc.
            On the streets:
            Fords/ Chevey's
crawl the hot tar.

V.

Cutthroat artist racing the night: "cocksucker,
            cocksucker, cocksucker!" she
shouts to mother hubbard as she dances the war
            dance of her hangout, Broken Bow.
Grand Canyon blues, "another day another dollar,"
sez the Meat Man, who does final   ly consent to sissy's
            surface wishes. "Horny?"
"You bitch you . . . you know I'll bust you."
The odor of Bar B Q/ of piss in the gutter
chitterlings/   shanks.
"I don't know how much longer I can take this shit."

Bank Pres.: "Yes sir, now tell me a little about
                             your past experience."
A machine working night and day/ telling lies
for a group of animals.
A hot dog dinner, a popcorn lunch/
A waitress goes to bed with a jackknife-faced guy.
She serves hamburgers like she's doing *it*.
"I thot Jesse James wuz the greatest hero I got,
      & I'd bet you you can't know why."
But the assistant under-secretary said: "We plan
        to drop the Bomb at zero hour."
"WHY?" too many communist/ old people's aid's expensive:
too many niggers around/ communist and niggers:
       too many too many

VI.

They scream down the halls of fame to us:
                 square! square! square!
    Down the depths:
                    hip! hip! the corny
bitch; the busted bastard/ the Jew with
his pawn shop/
the motherfuckers at the supermarket!
(the itch for junk . . . the twitch for life!
life) unrealized
"too many communists in this country lets hang niggers."
the peckerwoods murmur on their Ga., town steps.
CIA/ FBI/ Atom Bomb/ USA/)—"Fools rush in, where . . ."
—they said we could; undercover, uncover.
Discover: blow up; bomb out, protect . . . destroy.
Keep rats free in the cellar, running mad.
"Mama, buy me a bag of popcorn!" "O.K., but what do you
             want, Susan?" "I want a nigger, mama.
Please, may I . . . ?"
The colored girls of Harlem and South Side boost
        for the fix. For the Man, for Life.
Stripper strolling, bleached out, into happy arms.
Black heart builds against broken fury,
             running down her legs. The bum buys another
bottle: the Church is bombed, the lie is told.
Witches are burned, and the magic of the new man
        miles davis its way into beauty.

Poem to a Funky Night

In the red bar a maniac
plays & we clap. Numb
      with his riff where
    planets crash a-
cross Heaven his note comes
      through.
Oh we pick up. Hear the
jazz of a
universe. It's these wet streets
spangled with lights . . . Shlop! our feet
are walking.
    Reality is
what I feel and will
all Puritan get a red hot
fix. Humpty Dumpty.
      Your rabbit
bops w/ your spade princess: two
    in one, we high-
tail around a May Pole. Sweat
for our Angel our hands swing
at our sides. Oh
      will they touch once.
   In the meet.
      It is immortal
& all we have, sweet princess   Please
lift your face up
    high with love.

July 1963

Dances

Down Columbus Avenue:
    (no horses)-simonized Cadillac convertibles
    carrying paper flowers, Madonnas made of painted
    plaster,
    & banners hang from the door handles.

        The Majorette
is 12, breastless; her knees
are greased with salt & dirt.
        The sun
illuminates the cheap silk,
illustrates the gold &
thin black hairs upon her legs
& arms. Followed

by the North Beach Junior High School R.O.T.C.
                        BRASS Auxiliary Band:
paratroopers stomping through Roma,
holding tubas, trumpets, drums. Followed

  by the St. Francis Parochial Girls School Percussion Band
  in yellow & green silk & braid. The girls
  with their drums: snare, bass, kettle
  & triangle, cymbals)

        Not for a parade, the music-
         but for the dance! *Jubilate*
    Deo omnis terra!
    Puncta! puncta/ puncta

    bhm/ bhm/ bhm/

        (passed the Dunkit Donut Shop.
The tigers in their d.a. hairsets, sit, drink
coffee, Coke, & smoke their cigarettes; looking
        out the window for the young girls
who will walk by. The jukebox)

        Regular measure. Beat
of the dance. *Estampie,* the dance

filling the court with sound:
fiddles, trumpets, shawm, & viol.

Tumblers & acrobats! Jugglers
flinging porcelain balls
into the apex of a vaulted roof.

BEAN A DEMON ! (ROCK
A BABY! ROCK A BABY! ROCK A BABY BYE!
Yeah.   Motorcycle, S.F.P.D.,
pulls against the curb.
Black uniform, white crash-helmet,
walk into the Dunkit Donut Shop.) . . .

bhm/ puncta/ bhm
LOOK, the caravan
breaks camp; begins again, moving
through night (Bird's-eye-
high!) Tinder boxes clack
against the moving wagons: soft lights.
From here—with the hawk's wingtip
tickling my cheek—it looks
like a reel of unwound stars
going into the forest. The trees
hide everything from the birds.

If You Saw a Negro Lady

If you saw a Negro lady
sitting on a Tuesday
near the whirling doors of
Horn & Hardart on the main drag
of downtown Brooklyn

solitary and conspicuous as plain
and neat as walls impossible to
fresco and you watched her self
conscious features shape about
a Horn & Hardart teaspoon
with a pucker from a cartoon

she would not understand
with spine as straight and solid
as her years of bending over floors
allowed

skin cleared of interest by a ruthless
soap nails square and yellow-clean
from metal files

sitting in a forty-year-old flush
of solitude and prickling
from the new white cotton blouse
concealing nothing she bathed and ever noticed
even when she bathed and never
hummed a bathtub tune nor knew one

If you saw her square
above the dirty

mopped on antiseptic floors
before the rag-wiped table tops

little finger broad and stiff
in heavy emulation of a cockney
mannerism

would you join with her
on this occasion turn this treat
into surprise encourage
her performance by observing

happy birthday?

Musica
(for Woody Guthrie)

Sitting on the old running board
in the dust bowl
out out out Jesus in the night
out out out Moses in a cactus bush
out out out riding in my car car
out out out with children to follow you
out out out with Ghosts to dance with you
Sitting on the old running board
in the dust bowl
before television sets destroyed our hearts
out out out as the figures in black assemble
out out out riding in my car car
out out out the Jews come too
out out out liberation is a one word sword of peace
out out out suspenders dance in the far away Moon
out out out the Sioux and Cherokee are called Niggers
out out out Mark Twain driving a trailer truck full of
Cuban tobacco.
out out out on the stage a young Negro singing
out out out the Pope eating sandwiches and wine
out out out the Nazi with the tired stick
out out out the shoe shine prince on his knees in a
Poughkeepsie bar.
Out out out the miner has a crippled Son
out out out the professor has a sore tooth in January
out out out the tangerine dwarf seeks lemon drops for his
little daughter.
out out out into the wilderness past America, Oklahoma, past
Siberian teeth marks in the night
out out out riding in my car car
the dust covers the ancient windows
out out out Jesse James with his boots on
out out out Marlon Brando once again on a bike
out out out Joan kissing the Moon of honey
out out out Hungarian strip-teasers eating bananas
Sitting on the old running board i see You
with the guitar of a million caves and camps and mines
and shacks
and pines

and slaves
and children
and old nurses
and crippled runners
out out out
riding in my car car
with our windows open
smelling America
we often feel like speeding up and passing
but it wouldn't be right for two Ghosts
reliving a legend.

Second Coming

I

I see you,
woman of America
  standing with child
    heavy in the afternoon.
Dangerous eyes in a dark face,
  slowly rubbing the swollen belly
    feeling the kick of life
                      under your palms.
To what bloody future
  do you swear this emerging egg,
what terrible messiah will burst
 from the famous curve of your loins
to tear the crosses from the walls
and raise mighty arms in praise of himself?

II

Dominus vobiscum.
Dominus go frisk 'em.
Shake 'em down, god, they might have
something dangerous hidden in their
ragged coats,
these fire-headed youth scrambling under
your shocked and wary eyes,
these angry lambs whose only truth is now,
and only sin is love.
You fear their love,
        and rightly
for it is their very compassion
                for the living
that will hang you on the cross of
your own making,
and leave your corpse rotting in
                tomorrow's air.
Sancti, sancti, sancti,
the sheep of the streets
  with wolves in their bellies.

III

Anger and fear,
like blood and ice.
Anger thickening in the air
of sorrow,
and fear melting in the sun of tears.
I sing death to you, king.
My words like a common butcher's
knife slash through your ears.
You don't want to hear me,
for I have knelt at the altar of the
black mass,
and chanted your name in a curse,
that you might feel the fire you unleash
from places of hiding.
I call for the weeping sun and the
exploding air to find you cowering,
and carry you to the darkening fields
of your church,
for your own vultures to dip their
                    savage beaks
        into the dust of your soul,
and shriek with untamed feeding in the
                    roaring dawn,
until the calm of noon shall find flowers
                    sprouting
again in
the canyons of America.

Freda Norton

Cop-Out Court—Houston

MISS FREDA   I SHO GOT ME A BREAK
            THEY LET ME COP FER TWENTY-FIVE.
A BREAK! MY GOD MAN, WHY DID YOU TAKE   25 YEARS?

IT AIN'T SO BAD . . . I'M LUCKY!
            I KILLED ME A MAN   CAUSE
            HE WERE FUCKIN WITH MY WOMAN
            AND MESSING WITH MY LIFE.

WAS IT SELF-DEFENSE?

            WELL HE WANTED MY WIFE AND
            I LOVES MY WOMAN
            SO I TOOK THAT NIGGER'S LIFE!

(IN SILENCE I THOUGHT, WHAT CAN I SAY?)

            THIS TIME HE SAID FREDA
            I CAN BE OUT IN A FEW YEARS
            IF I BE GOOD. WHY, IN JANUARY
            MY CELL MATE GOT THE CHAIR
            FOR MURDER SAME CHARGE AS MINE
            AND IN FEBRUARY ANOTHER CELL MATE
            GOT NINE-NINE. I WAS SCARED
            TO FIGHT IN THIS WHITE MANS COURT
            CAUSE . . . MAN,
            I AIN'T SORRY I KILLED THAT NIGGER.
            HE THREW MY WOMAN IN A DITCH
            AND HAD HER THEN AND THERE.
            WE GOT FIVE CHILLEN, ME AND HER, AND
            WELL . . . HE HAD TO DIE. SOMEHOW
            I HAD TO SAVE HER HONOR.
            MY WOMAN'S BLACK. . . . NO COURT
            WOULD TAKE HER SERIOUS. THEY SAYS,
            NIGGERS ALWAYS FUCK AND FIGHT.
            SO I DIDN'T RISK A JURY, I COPPED
            FER TWENTY-FIVE.

WHAT YOU THINK FREDA   AIN'T I
                A LUCKY MAN ?   I WOULD HAVE NEVER
                MAKE A JURY UNDERSTAND.

YES, I GUESS YOU DID THE WISEST THING
                AND I SWALLOWED HARD BEFORE I ASK
                this MAN, what is your name   ?
                then they called me to go and i
                left GEORGE in lock-up. gave him
                my cigarettes   was all that i
                could do,   but he knew i understood.

COP-OUT COURT   NEXT !
                this won't take but a minute . . .

African Memories
(for the Watusi in their hour of need)

they are fighting, she
sd, on the beaches, etc.

and on the left flank, a
small detachment of batwas,
poison dart blowguns eveready
as batteries. for three centuries
the bourgeoisie held subjugated
to the artists, merely because
of height. the lovely air
one breathes when one is
seven feet tall. keep them
down, damn them, but are
there beaches in ruanda?

listen, all over the region
the drums are beating, bahutus
rage, seethe, form into
companies the lion invented
the assegai just when napoleon
ravaged the continent.   hah!
where were the bahutus damn
them when humphrey sailed down
the river?   and needed them,
even to some fermented native
juice to replace the gin she
poured away, bitch.   but they
sunk it anyway.   altho the
konigsberg did make it upriver,
that was somewhere else in
africa.   but they, the krauts,
dismounted the twelve inch guns
and hauled them inland.   the last
german force to surrender, two
or three weeks after armistice day.

so there they are, spread
against the indian ocean, the
arabian sea, the mediterranean,
the south atlantic, fighting

all these years away. but for
three hundred years the artists
were ahead, by virtue of their
impossible height, and the togas
they wore draped shoulder to hip.

arise!   formez vos bataillons!
on to the dark continent!

From Visiting a Dead Man on a Summer Day

In flat America, in Chicago,
Graceland cemetery on the German north side.
Forty feet of Corinthian candle
celebrate Pullman embedded
lonely raisin in a cake of concrete
almost as far below.
The Potter Palmers float
in an island parthenon.
Barons of hogfat, railroads and wheat
are postmarked with angels and lambs.

But the Getty tomb: white, snowpatterned
in a triangle of trees
swims dappled with leaf shadow,
sketched light arch within arch
delicate as fingernail moons.

The green doors should not be locked.
Doors of fern and flower should not be shut.
Louis Sullivan, I sit on your grave.
It is not now good weather for prophets.
Sun eddies on the steelsmoke air like sinking honey.
The green doors should stand open
and the body lie face up
loose in the earth
so the rain can trickle through.

On the inner green door of the Getty tomb
(a thighbone's throw from your stone)
a marvel of growing, blooming, thrusting into seed:
how all living wreathe and insinuate
in the circlet of repetition that never repeats:
ever new birth never rebirth.
Each tide pool microcosm
form the free spiraling of your hand.

Box that dances,
light tomb of laughter and spores . . .

Thirty years in the vast rumbling gut
of this society you stormed
to be used, screamed
no louder than any other breaking voice.
The waste of a good man
bleeds the future that's come
in Chicago, in flat America
where the poor still bleed from the teeth
housed in sewers and filing cabinets,
where prophets may spit into the wind
till anger sleets their eyes shut,
where this house that dances the seasons
and the braid of all living
and the joy of a man making his new good thing,
is strange, irrelevant as a meteor,
In Chicago, in flat America
In this year of our burning.

Poor White

Nowadays
a whiteman's job in the Southern Appalachians
can keep rickets out of the kids
but not the worms; keep Tb off the wife
but not the neighbors; keep a man going
60 hrs a week for a season
but not for life.
Yet better off than slumdwellers,
a better man, he thinks, than any Negro,
he fixes the hate he bred into him
first on kids, wife mules and red clay hills,
then learns to harangue
the violence in him with tobacco and moonshine
and long rides on bloodshot midnights
after standing in town with the crowd
that has stood there for a century now
listening to the barcarolles of politicians,
the keening of huckster revivalists,
the bullshit of supremacists,
who own the land and him.

Gyre's Galax

Sound variegated through beneath lit
Sound variegated through beneath lit
through sound beneath variegated lit
sound variegated through beneath lit

Variegated sound through beneath lit dark
Variegated sound through beneath lit dark
sound variegated through beneath lit
variegated sound through beneath lit dark

Through variegated beneath sound lit
Through variegated beneath sound lit
through beneath lit
through beneath lit
through beneath lit
Thru beneath
Thru beneath
Thru beneath
Thru beneath
Thru beneath lit

Twainly ample of amongst
Twainly ample of amongst
Twainly ample of amongst
in lit black viewly
                viewly
          in viewly
                viewly
          in viewly
                viewly
          in viewly
                viewly
in lit black viewly
in dark to stark

in dark to stark
in dark to stark
in dark to stark
in dark to stark lit

In above beneath
    above beneath lit
    above beneath
    above beneath lit
    above beneath
    above beneath
    above beneath
    above beneath
    above beneath lit

Poem No Name Fits

We have come that far over and
much more said
                    done
the complete circle docilely whole no
torn rim to scrape bone, our
wheel straight on its
course, no rough edges, that's it no

slicing away at breasts buttocks

hiking up between the legs cunt or balls
that tenderest of places as
my father said
                    hit 'em there
if there's trouble don't wait let 'em
have it on the spot
there where it counts and i

think now of the breasts
served up by civil guards
in spain those mummified arms the
turks used to beat their galley slaves
                                        sade's
shitting monk and hitler's lampshades not
to mention endless parts just
withering from hunger or
alone. alone is as well
a desecration, two being the
whole one the
whole thing, being
what we have come for are
coming from and towards. whether we
eat or not
there's another question and
no one's father or mother asks that one and
no one answers, too busy
making pain killers those priests.

Lennox Raphael

Sidewalk Blues

upturn cunt city smooth with laughter
laugh in the sidewalk eyes
            till god comes
with a gush of amorphous happiness
in the junkieloopers of the dead gyrating sadness
                pocketed in the benevolent anus
                atop the empire state building

            trying to goose the world's fair
city i am the laughter and the laugh and the dog
                an exterminator between my legs
                with kaleidoscopes of flesh
                burning cloves in the eyes
as you walk uptown
            (coming downtown with filth in your nostrils)
you look up
and the sky is a corpse

        that stands and pisses on a wornout jesuschrist

the sky says amen and children are raped
                by anthropomorphic policemen in spacesuits
                policemen paid to slaughter pregnant women
                and eat the little startlings torn out of their tummies
                blessed with the cassock of fungus
where is the eye that sees the sidewalk in throbbing agony
                as death passes on a fishbone
                hooked to its fly
                    (open as the gate to hell)
                and garlanded with the flowers left by inept poets
who imitate german typewriters
                and eat the flesh of their contemporaries

            atop the empire state building
the city is the father of the slum
                and the slummedup cunt is now bereft
                of its
                    IBM clitoris

or the pleasure of wall-street brokers
    (men of reason and non-reason)
vho employ policemen to watch their daughters deflowered
    by security-bearing sugardaddies

he slum walks with a swagger
nd little tinsels of faith are left
    on the sidewalk

fficers of the rent rehabilitation center take these
insels to the mayor
vho
    (in spurts of irrational courage)
urns them in national conventions
    so happy landlords (with the slum expanding and
    business coming downtown)
ponsor poetry readings for coldwater poets in need of
    supermarket sperm
    oh where is the lie on the sidewalk
ruths are without form
    and they have no legs
o walk from town to town
    looking up and down
or pennies in the gutter
lready dragged by sanitation engineers
    looking for the bits and pieces of little negroes

    eaten by policemen
vorking for the office of extermination

    (flowers are beautiful
    but nostrils draw insects
    from their cores)

vhere are the desperate people who walk the streets
    with flat tires in their bellybuttons
vhere are the ones who sanction the slaughter
    when the air becomes thick
    and candles go out
    slamming the doors behind them
h the cap is on the eye and the cunt is hid with laughter
    in the eye of the hurricane

nodding in doorways of the disemboweled ideas
floating about in coffeehouses and fishingboats

oh the captain is the diaphragm salesman
        going from house to house on the american continent
fitting pt boats
        and young housewives
who ache between the legs for judas
        sucking blind men in street-clothes selling pins
and needles
and holding the hands of the dead
        atop
      the burning sperm
as the dome collapses and the city crashes its airports
        on policemen

with fragmentary dicks in their nostrils

oncemore upon a time the city goes down and god comes up
        with a religious erection
        ramcrammed with survivors
shorn of their sexes and lips and tongues and intestines
        and hearts and minds and ignorance

and god takes them to the empire state building
and a bolt of lightning severs his erection
and survivors float away on bits and pieces
        of congealed sperm
bought beforehand
        at horn and hardart
then the thunder came and the rain came and the flood came
        and the sun shone
and the president came out of his shelter
        in Marlboro country
looked around and saw the ruins of his imagination
returned to the shelter with his dogs
          and his birds
called another president on the hot line
        and said

        thy kingdom come thy will be done
and the apes and the dogs and the cows came out

          of cathedrals
and their civilization grew on four legs
and there was no more need for crutches
and rapists and embezzlers of the mind
for
there was disorganization throughout the land
                                                    and
god ruled the atheists
forever and ever   amen

then a cow stepped on a bomb in a supermarket
              and the civilization became ashes
              and god came out of the earth
a stick of pot between his teeth   and rubbers on his sex
              digging the scene

and on the third day he went to the world's fair
              with abraham lincoln at his side

              holding an umbrella over his sex
              and waving to the skeletons uptown

while
      (downtown)
the garment district was naked with fear
                                              atop
          the empire state building
                                              where
i now stop.

David Rasey

Sounds of Buddy Tate

In this city of many offerings,
        among friends I have not yet met
Your face, New York,   jazz wails
through the garden of The Museum
Of Modern Art.

Through and in the flesh/ spirit
bodies beneath building of
Hart Crane structure.

Buildings, tall concrete
somehow,   wait
for jazz sound,
from green-sculptured garden
below.

Stone waits people wait
soon It will begin.
These rhythms, my rhythms
This city, my sound of jazz

The jazz fever heats
        the many faces
but still there is no sound—
O God let the beat begin.

It begins, Lord Sweet It begins.

Move baby in/out heads bobbin'
Move in/out in/out
Wail movin'   Sound-jazz
hands clappin'   bodies swayin'

Work tenor sax Talk

All all All, All
movin', sweet beat go
there there there
You've got us

we, the children of jazz
we are your culture

We hear/feel your sermon.

The Jackal-Headed Cowboy

We were - clinging to our aboreal - rustled
by a poplin dude so fast that even now
we mistake big mack trucks flying
confederate crossbones for rompaging
steer, leaping into their sandpaper hides
and lassoing their stobble faced drivers as they roar into
corn flaked greasy spoons.

We span the spic and spanned cesspools
nerves rankling like hot headed guerillas
bayoneting artery routes and crawling through
our bowels with blades in their teeth.

Our mohair suits, our watches, our horn
rimmed glasses and several telephones
petition us to slow down as we forget
whose soupcan we swim.

We stand at Brooklyn Bridge like
mayakovsky before, deafened by the nuts
and bolts and clogged in the comings and
goings of goings of Usura

We are homesick weary travelers in the
jungian sense and miss the brew of the
long night's pipe.

Our dreams point like bushy mavericks to
hawking game and scattering ripple falls.
We will swing from giant cables as if
they were hemp, hacking away at sky
scrapers til they tumble into christmas
crowds.
We will raid chock full O nuts untying
apron strings crouching stealthily in the streets
breaking up conference rooms sweeping away
forms memo pads, ransoming bank presidents
shoving dollar bills through their mahogany
jaws.
We will sit on Empire Sofas listening to

Gabrieli's fortissimo trumpets blare for
stewed and staggering Popes as Tom Tom mallets
beat the base of our brains.
We will leap tall couplets in a single bound
and chant chant Chant until our pudgy swollen
lips go on strike.
Our daughters will shake rattle roll and slop
snapping their fingers until grandfather
clocks' knees buckle and Tudor mansions free
their cobwebs.
Our mothers will sing shout swing and foam
making gothic spires get happy clapping the
night like blown up Zeppelin.

We will sizzle burn crackle and fry like combs
snapping the naps of Henri Christopher's daughters.
and We will scramble breasts bleating like
some tribe run amuck up and down desecrating
cosmotological graveyard factories.
and We will mash stock exchange bugs til
their sticky brown insides spill out like
reams of ticker tape.
and We will drag off yelling pinching bawling
shouting pep pills, detergents, acne powders,
clean rooms untampered maiden heads finger bowls
napkins renaissance glassware time subscriptions
reducing formulas
- please call before visiting -
- very happy to make your acquaintanceship i'm sure -
and boil down one big vat of unanimal stew
topped with kegs and kegs of whipped dynamite
and cheery smithereens.
and then We will rush like crazed antelopes
with our bastard babies number books mojo goober
dusting razor blades chicken thighs spooky ha'nts
daddygracing fatherdivining jack legged preaching
bojangles sugar raying mamas into one scorching
burning lake and have a jigging hoedown with the
Quadrilling Sun.
and the panting moneygrabbing landlord
leeching redneck judges will scuffle
the embankment and drag the lipstick sky outside.

and their fuzzy patriarchs from Katzenjammer orphic
will offer hogmaws and the thunder bird and their overseers
will offer elixir bottles of pre punch cards
and the protocol hollering thunder will announce
our main man who'll bathe us and swathe us.
and Our man's spur jingles 'll cause the clouds to
kick the dust in flight.
And his gutbucketing rompity bump will
cause sweaty limp flags to furl retreat
and the Jackal-headed cowboy will ride reins
whiplashing his brass legs and knobby hips.
And fast draw Anubis with his crank letters from Ra
will Gallop Gallop Gallop

our mummified profiled trail boss
as our swashbuckling storm fucking mob rides shot
gun for the moon and the whole seiged stage coach
of the world will heave and rock as we
bang stomp shuffle stampede cartwheel and cakewalk our
way into Limbo.

From Poems

I

i am busy now sawing my leg off,
i have localized my self hate,
i sliced my head precisely in half and placed a strainer
inside, that did not work,
i nailed myself to a turning tractor rotor,
that did not work,
i invented a machine that would tear women's nipples off,
i tore open a new mother's stitches as she screamed,
i kicked in the head of every infant who crawled near me,
i stuck pencils into her eyes and twisted,
i severed the penis off every boy child i could find,
i burned their balls over my fire and ate them,
i hated them,
i murdered them over and over,
i starved them and ate what was left,
i hated them,

II

i am love,
i am beauty,
i am goodness,
i do not hate them anymore,
i hate only my leg.

4

summary

no sleep tonight
not even after all
the red and green pills
i have pumped into
my stuttering self or
the sweet wine
that drowns them.
                              this is
a poem for the world
for the slow suicides
in seclusion.
somewhere on 130th st.
a woman, frail as a
child's ghost, sings. oh
                          oh. what
can the matter be? johnny's
so long at the fair.
                          /i learned how
                                to masturbate
thru the new york times

i thought
shd i have
thought anything
that cd not
be proved.
i thought and
all that.
will not change
was wrong. listen.
                                    fool
                black
                          bitch
of fantasy. life
is no more than
                          gents
                                and
                                      gigolos (99% american)
            liars

        and
        killers (199% american)   dreamers
                                          and
                                          drunks (299% american)

(ONLY GOD IS 300% AMERICAN)
                      i say
is everybody happy?
this is a poem for me
i am alone.
one night of words
will not change
all that.

Poem from Jail

. . .And I have crawled
        thru the forest
        near the Doom's Day Machine,
        puking blood
        & clutching guts,
        And I have clutched
        my Amulet, Ammonite,
        for dreams,
        & have used
        my sacred slab
        of Voidal Concretions
        as pillow
        & have clutched
        my scrolls,
        & have held
        the covenant of my mind
        and certain artifacts,
        as sacred,
        and have notched
        my staff with
        the times,
        & have clothed
        the body with
        feathers from
        the Bevy of Birds,
& my arms thrust
        themselves out
        of feathers,
        prick dangles
        out of feathers,
        head barfs itself
        out of feathers;
        on my feet are
        sandals,
        in my heart
        is a ravenous Duck;
        & I have laid bare
        my choice-patterns,
        freaked in the
        shit of Being,

& I am laid
bare in the
                Burning Bush,
& have pissed
out of the holly leaves,
& I am innocent
& my whiteness
is as the
whiteness of the Lamb.
And we have
seen the men
farting around
in Geneva,
and the governments
have not clasped
one another
as lovers,
shedding the
buffer-zones,
confronting
each other
in Nakedness.
No, they have
not halted hate.
Yes, it is true;
Death shall assume
the continuum.
if I am turned
to atomic death
here in my cell,
Let I leave behind
for earthologists
a masturbation,
poetry on
toilet tissue,
love-body of
continuing
nonviolence;
and I shall
project myself
to that time
where I am
clad in feathers,

& my mind
is ejaculated
into the Cosmos,
& I breathe
the god-breath,
& dance
in the rays
of Nonviolence,
staring into forever.

Atman

i fed an Indian boy
once in Madras.
bought him a meal
at the Y
consisting of curry
chappati, dahl and ghee. -
he ate so rapidly
that the luxury of silverware
was an impediment
which he cast aside
preferring his right hand
as usual, as he scooped up
the food in mounds
and shoveled it into
his vacuum mouth rapid fire. -
then he proceeded to tell me:
"I have five brother, four sister,
and a mother and father, -
all hungry."
afterwards he stood outside
waiting and waiting until
i emerged and was fallen upon
by twenty to thirty
of his friends
all hungry-wanting-waiting
limping around in broken
dance-many sprawled

maimed or rotting in the streets.
I made my way followed and
latched onto by hordes of
the ragged, dirty, hungry
and impoverished
some not able to walk
twenty feet - all crying
"Naye pesa, naye pesa"
in that haunting revelation
of need -
Then i entered a bus

protected by a sympathizer
who said, "Beggars, go away."
whereupon one threw some dirt
through the window and most
motioned right hand
spasmodically to
swollen or non existent
stomach and then to
parched mouth
all demanding manna
or naye pesa
or another two hours
of life.

Sunglasses

The shield
The breakaway from reality
The shield
The ugly movements of people
The shield
Green
The shield
Blindness
The shield
Death!
The shield
Sunglasses!!

Isiah Smith

Church on the Corner of Union and Third

As I was walking not especially wanting not especially
    caring no particular place in mind
        only for me just to walk
And before I knew it I was in front of this
                cathedral-like structure
Builted real high way up there like
              with a clock on top
    with faces that look at you from four different
ways
    and bells that ring the time for those who
        are blind to the march of
              time

it is called
      a catholic church and it is for catholic
           people
   and the birds that fly around
   and nest in its steeple are even
           catholic birds
   upon this church I will build my home you know
   like thats for the birds
And you know many many people attend this church
and if you would see them
          they look like ants before
           a big rain looking for a
             hole
    seeking shelter from the sins of the world
    but now no one is inside it is real
          quiet and empty
all except for this man standing
quietly in front ragged out in black
   this stud is called a priest
   and he just stands silently reading his
   Holy Book
        praying I think for all of
              us

and really looking like he is concerned
   and I think he like the rest has been and still are
   shucking the mass with all that jive
      but don't he know that a
    great awakening is taking place

He may mean well but he is asleep
                    and but he don't sleep alone
                        why don't he open his eyes so
the rest might see
                    only him just stand there
            quietly reading his Holy Book
            and looking real concerned
                            with a dolorous
                    expression
                        on his face

while the birds that fly high around the steeple
and one selected fly down and shit at his
                                feet
        as a token of their highest esteem
so I walk on by not saying a thing
                        a token of my high
                                esteem
            And then he turns and walks away
            and I say perhaps he is going glue
                        himself in front
                            of his T.V. and see
        Just how much him and the likes of
            him are doing for the world
            and so I walk on and as I look back
            I can't help but wonder why the
clock is not striking the hour when it is plain to see
                but it is behind time
                            and empty quiet
        and lonely
                and looking like its up for sale.

Clee Snipe, Jr.

Black Backlash

Who do you like Charlie?
The Vietcong or me
I like vanilla ice cream
But you can't jive me over Manila

Going to Chicago sorry but you can't move next to me
Viola Liuzzo a white soul sister murder by trick law
Damn!   a sincere white mother ain't even worth a plug
nickel anymore.

Shit! give me another civil rights bill
I want to get super charged up so I can think like
C. Wright Mills

Bang! Bang! Beep! Beep!

Fulbright and Morse code two voices in the wilderness
dying of thirst.
Dig Baby! now that's not nice to call for a hearse.

Gona have a party! Halloween is here again
Trick or Treat!
No! No! No! I think the Hawks are going to take escalation
soup with French Fries.

I Play Flute
(for Bob)

where
in all
the awful
apparatus
we acquired
to hasten
freedom
is
the
flute

the
fine
thin
flute
the flute
thin
thing
the
thin
thin
thing
which
thinner
than
the
rain
rings
freedom
in

Lady Day Spring-Toned

                         april-warmly
                         blue-sky-silently
"Heart in my soul
has got this solo"
                         overhead
                         overheard

Charley Parker-birds
(a-flat minor fart-
ing perfume
of magenta smell
from a far corner
of a microcosmic universe)
stand still
In nowhere air
Lady Day's heart
in her soul
(21-dimensionless-
dimension overtones
from 5 dimensional
Pagliacci scenes
we see only 3 dimensionally)
                         solos
Phony American Charley Morality
ate my flesh
but my soul was
West of horizons to
phony American Charley Morality
Everybody knows trouble
double-trouble
triple-trouble
I've seen
like a motherless child
traveling light
through 5 dimensional scenes
foolish fools
see as 3 dimensional
I hungered for you're -my-
thrill-don't-explain love (no, don't explain love)
I thirsted for easy-living-
for-you-love

Trying to find love
found me pain
trying to give love
gave me pain
Spikes spiking skin pain
swarms of insects stinging pain
Starfire pain
burning in every pore
burning every blood vessel
burning in every bone's marrow
Pain eating like cancer
Pain screaming so loud it's silent
I'm gone now
I'm gone how
Wow I'm gone
21st heaven melody!
Wink-smile-wink rhythm
Cosmic harmony
All 3 bound me
in future futureless
silent sounds
I've found
Love's strange fruits
in some other spring
where no pain sings
here in nowhere

Gloria Tropp

Poem for Ernie Henry

paint my crib a
                          land of grass . . . . scarabs & mariposas
holy hour
                     in the city . . . in the aisles of oil & perfumes
my lids part the people dressed in strings
                                    wearing tensions
                          making dances come through
                                             longing
GOD'S SELF of straw of straw burning on both
                                    ends
                               WHAT! WHAT! WHAT!
and WHAT foot glides through days that are ONE SCREAM
                          LOUDER THAN THE NEXT
Body light making blues offering

                               under a low range of sky
and other blues
                     in a coat . . . . that dims blues ears
and WHAT WHAT for my blues . . . .
                               all the world that's

                                                  a
                                             tree

engraved on the cheek of facing
                          this hard stone

Stephen Tropp
Howard Hart

From To Jackie in Jail

Your hands are envelopes for a wet velvet stump
You went to the doctor your thumbs exploding
And the green blood rained white through a jail
                              in Payan Wisconsin
Incest and masturbation the girl with the face of
                                        a deer
                    ran away with the curtains
Jackie what are dreams worth when a pin means heaven
                                              Jackie
The yellow blood on the white thighbone screamed
                      for the conflagrations of the rain
And a dog shouted the alphabet using only chinese scales

II.

You were never really hooked you never stayed out of jail
                              long enough
Born in an elephant's black tooth Jackie you invented
                                      a prison

                              out of licorice poles
The legends of the east are unlike any other
From your twentieth floor cell your tongue of radium and
                                              nettles
                    incited Bennington girls to riot
Big enough to squint you fought four fans saying you were
                                              the only
                    Napoleon born in Calcutta you shot
Nerve patterns from the blood's skylight
Human beings with four feet and the sound of being alive
                              to nothing at all
Jackie how tall is a beanstalk when does the rainbow die

III.

SCREAM JACKIE   DREAM JACKIE
solve the trigonometry of the heart with air streams
                                    and pink wax I know
That this is not the country   TO HELL
With your God damned Africa   My skin has feathers
You bought the first helicopter and landed in our laps
And the English boys with hashish in their diapers
                              passed out German bennies
Six at a time that was no hypo that was my heart that was my
                                                       belt

IV.

And what are stars but a kind of fan club for the juvenile
                        delinquents of 116th street
Jackie Jackie what happened when the cop said the streets
                                                    are
                        just one oblong toilet
JACKIE   JACKIE   JACKIE   JACKIE
On piano bass guitar
On vibes flugelhorn
On blackberries and xylophone
On horse I sold ermine gloves to Lady Godiva and you Jackie
                                                       out
On a rhinoceros climbed the walls of the chandeliers of
                                    my opera
                        by Puccini . . .

Love Poem to the Magician

The scarves
            none . . .
            chrysanthemums come tumbling
            down your sleeves,
the teeth of your special mouth biting a rain-
            drop in two
      spitting out the hulls
a magnet in your breast pulls my
                  blood vessels loose
ties them
            at the throat
                  together

                  George Washington & I went to your show
                  sat in the audience
                  waiting for the famous act
                  you made the Delaware River
                  appear
                  you made Mt. Vernon
                  appear
                  You made a flag wave
                  in mid air
But oh Mr. Magician, most of all
                  you
      turned me into a different woman
            one who could
make tables move with only the
                  blood pulse
moving in my white white wrist.

Poetry

I've got to be honest. I can
make good word music and rhyme

at the right times and fit words
together to give people pleasure

and even sometimes take their
breath away—but it always

somehow turns out kind of phony.
Consonance and assonance and inner

rhyme won't make up for the fact
that I can't figure out how to get

down on paper the real or the true
which we call life. Like the other

day. The other day I was walking
on the lower exercise yard here

at San Quentin and this cat called
Turk came up to a friend of mine

and said Ernie, I hear you're
shooting on my kid. And Ernie

told him So what, punk? And Turk
pulled out his stuff and shanked

Ernie in the gut only Ernie had a
metal tray in his shirt. Turk's

shank bounced right off him and
Ernie pulled his stuff out and of

course Turk didn't have a tray and
caught it dead in the chest, a bad

one, and the blood that came to his
lips was a bright pink, lung blood,

and he just laid down in the grass
and said Shit. Fuck it. Sheeit.

Fuck it. And he laughed a long time
time, softly, until he died. Now

what could consonance or assonance or
even rhyme do with something like that?

BIOGRAPHICAL NOTES

Daisy Aldan was born in New York in 1923. Her poems have appeared in *Poetry* (Chicago), *The Massachusetts Review,* and many other magazines. Her recent books include: *The Masks Are Becoming Faces,* Maryland, 1965; *The Destruction of Cathedrals,* New York, 1965; *A Bell Is Not a Bird,* El Corno Emplumado Press, Mexico, and Seven-Seven, New York, 1966, in which "Yorkville" is included. It was first published in *El Corno Emplumado.*

Bob Allen was born in 1942 in Atlanta, Georgia, and is now living in New York. Currently studying sociology at the New School for Social Research. "Musical Vietnams" appeared in *Poets of Today* (Berlin, 1967).

Carol Bergé was born in 1928 in New York City. Her work has appeared in *The Nation, Origin, Poetry, Yale Literary Magazine* and other magazines; and in the following anthologies: *Four Young Lady Poets* (Totem/Corinth, New York, 1962); *Of Poetry and Power* (Basic Books, New York, 1963); *Erotic Poetry, Classic to Contemporary* (Random House, New York, 1963) and *Poems Now* (Kulchur Press, New York, 1966). "Chant for Half the World" appeared in *Notes from Underground* (California, 1960).

Art Berger was born in 1920 in New York. A printer and sailor, his essays and poems have been published in many magazines, including *Fiddlehead, Mainstream, Liberation* and *Umbra,* of which he is a contributing editor. His book *Blow the Man Down* was published by Poetry (London/New York, 1962). "March on the Delta" appeared in *American Dialog.*

Paul Blackburn was born in Vermont in 1926. A former Fulbright scholar, he was poetry editor of *The Nation* in 1961. His work has appeared in *New American Poetry* and numerous magazines and anthologies. His recent books include *Brooklyn-Manhattan Transit* (1960); *The Nets* (1961); *Poems for Reardon* (Madison 1967); *The Cities* (Grove Press, N. Y., 1967).

Horace Julian Bond was born in 1940 in Atlanta, where he has been a civil rights activist and was elected and seated in the Georgia state legislature. His poems have appeared in *American Negro Poetry* (N.Y., 1963) and other anthologies and magazines. "I, Too, Hear America Singing" appeared in *American Dialog.*

Grace Butcher was born in 1934 in Rochester, New York and now lives in Ohio. Her work has appeared in *American Weave, Trace, Midwest, Penny Papers* and many other magazines. She has had two books of poetry published: *The Bright Colored Dark* (Cleveland, 1966) and *More Stars Than Room For* (Ohio, 1966).

Harold Carrington was born in Atlantic City, where he died at the age of 25 in 1964. He spent most of his last ten years in jail, where he wrote all his poems. They are being prepared for publication.

Len Chandler was born in Ohio in 1935, and is now living in New York. He is widely known as a folksinger, composer and participant in civil rights demonstrations. He makes his appearance here as a poet in a section from a longer work, "21A." He has published in *Sing Out* and *Broadside.* Columbia has issued an album of his songs, *To Be a Man.*

Charlie Cobb was born in Washington, D. C., in 1944, and has been active in SNCC, Atlanta. His work has appeared in *The New Republic, Liberation* and other publications.

Kirby Congdon was born in 1924 in Pennsylvania and is now living in New York, where he edits *Interim Books* and *Magazine*. He is the author of *Iron Ark: A Bestiary* (Interim Books, 1962); *Juggernaut* (Interim Books, 1965) and *Dream-Work: Black Leather Fantasies* (Boss Books, 1967). His work has appeared in *London Times' Literary Supplement*, *Boss*, *City*, *Dare*, *American* and many other magazines. "Chorus for Phonograph" appeared in *El Corno Emplumado*, April, 1963, and is the opening section of a four-part work entitled "Aipotu."

Victor Hernandez Cruz was born in 1949, in Aguas Buenas, Puerto Rico; he is now living in New York. His work has appeared in *What's Happening*, *Insight Magazine* and *Ben Jay Flash*. "The Land" appears in his book *Papo Got His Gun* (Calle Once Publications, 1966, New York), and his most recent collection, *Snaps*, has just been published by Random House.

Wesley Day was born in 1935 in San Francisco; he now lives in New York. His work has appeared in *Epos*, *Poetry Review*, *Island* and many other magazines. His book *On To Me Now* was published in West Germany, 1959.

Allen De Loach is a native of Jacksonville, Florida, and is now living in Buffalo, where he edits the magazine *Intrepid*. His work has appeared in many magazines, including *Poet Meat*, *Wormwood Review*, *University of Tampa Poetry Review*.

Diane Di Prima, a native New Yorker, now lives in Kerhonkson, N.Y. Her poems and stories have appeared in many magazines and anthologies, including *Poems Now*. She edits the poetry news letter, *The Floating Bear*, and the *Poets Press*. Her books include *This Kind of Bird Flies Backward*, and *Dinners and Nightmares*, (N. Y., 1961). "Goodbye Nkrumah" appeared in *Intrepid*, 1966.

Ree Dragonette was born in 1918 in Philadelphia, Pennsylvania. She has published two pamphlets: *Like Pharaoh's Eye, Like Onyx Stone* (1962) and *With Brunt of Angels* (1965). Her poems have appeared in various magazines, including *Seventh Street Quarterly* and *Harper's Bazaar*.

Al Fowler was born in New York in 1939. His poems have appeared in *City Lights Journal #1, Fuck-You,* and *Intrepid,* where "Peyote Poem" was published.

A. Frederic Franklyn was born in 1927 in New York; he now works in Hollywood, California. He is editorial director of the International Press Bulletin and film editor of Trace. His work has appeared in *Let's Live, Duende, Coastlines, Impetus* and many other publications. His poem "Book Allargando" was included in *Necromancy Notebooks* and was published in the magazine *Duende* (Fall, 1964).

Carl Gardner was born in 1931 in Washington, D. C. His work has appeared in *Northwest Review, Patterns, Dasein* and in the anthologies *Beyond the Blues* and *New Negro Poets.*

Serge Gavronsky was born in 1932 in Paris, France, and has been a New York resident for a long time. His work has appeared in *Versatility in Verse* (Young Publishers, 1965); *Where Is Viet Nam?* and in the magazines *El Corno Emplumado, Wormwood Review, Things, Radex* and many others.

Barbara Gibson is a native of Wisconsin (born 1930); her poems have appeared in *Cheshire, The Other, Quixote.* Her books are: *Our Bedroom's Underground* (with Morgan Gibson) Milwaukee, 1963; *Say My Name,* La Crosse, 1967. "After the Quarrel" appeared in *Two by the Gibsons* (Milwaukee, 1966).

Emilie Glenn was born in 1932 in Paris, France, and is a longtime New York resident. Her poetry and stories have been published in the *Southwest Review, Massachusetts Review, Western Humanities Review, University of Kansas City Review, New Mexico Quarterly Review, Prairie Schooner* and many others.

John Harriman lives in New York, where he has participated in many poetry readings. His work has appeared in *Theo, Intrepid, The Seventh Street Anthology* and other publications.

Emily Catharine Harris was born in 1921 in Ithaca, New York. She is a painter who has published poems in *Anglo-Welsh Review* and *Wormwood Review*.

Howard Hart, a native of Ohio, has published two books: *Fountain Square* and *Sky of Orange*. His work has appeared in *Exodus, Beat Coast East* and other magazines. "To Jackie in Jail" appeared in *Intrepid #40*.

David Henderson was born in Harlem in 1942 and has been widely published in magazines, including *The National Guardian, Mainstream* and *Black American*. He is the editor of the magazine *Umbra*. His book *They Are Killing All the Young Men* was published by Poets Press.

Calvin C. Hernton was born in Tennessee in 1933. He is a sociologist now living in London. Doubleday, New York, has published his *Sex and Racism in America* and *White Papers for White Americans*. His poetry has appeared in a number of magazines and he is the author of *The Coming of Chronos to the House of Nightsong* (a volume of poetry).

Barbara Holland was born in 1925 in Portland, Maine. She is the author of *Return in Sagittarius* (Eventorium Press, 1965) and *A Game of Scraps* (Prarie Press, 1967). Her work has appeared in *Epos, Camel's Coming, Dust, Origins/Diversions, Simbolica, New Concepts* (England) and *Weed* (Canada), as well as many other magazines. "In Moloch's Eye" first appeared in *Kauri,* January, 1965, New York City.

Will Inman is a North Carolinian (born 1923) who has been active on the New York poetry scene for many years. He is the editor of *Kauri* and has been published in a number of magazines. His recent books include *I Am the Snake-Handler* (New Atheneum Press, 1960); *A River of Life* (New Atheneum Press, 1961) and *108 Prayers for J. Edgar,* Selections (1945). His poem "Kauri" appeared in the magazine *Kauri.*

Marvin Jackman was born in 1944 in Fowler, California. His works (poems, plays, essays) have appeared in *Soul Book,* and *Black Dialogue* magazine. His poem "Blues for Lucifer" appeared in the *Journal of Black Poetry.*

Gerald Jackson was born in Chicago in 1936. He now lives in New York City. He is a painter as well as a poet.

Joe Johnson lives in New York City. His poems have appeared in *Umbra, Liberator* and *Revolution Africaine.*

Percy Edward Johnston was born in New York in 1930. He is editor of *Dasein* and the author of *Concerto for Girl* and *Six-Cylinder Olympic.*

Lenore Kandel lives in San Francisco. Her poems have appeared in *Evergreen, Notes from Underground, San Francisco Review* and many other magazines. Her published books include: *A Passing Dragon* (Three-Penny Press, 1959); *An Exquisite Navel* (Three-Penny Press, 1959) and *The Love Book* (Stolen Paper Review Editions, 1966). Grove Press, New York, is publishing a volume of her poetry. "First They Slaughtered the Angels" was originally published in *The Beatitude Anthology* (1960).

Allen Katzman was born in 1937 in Brooklyn. He is an editor of *East Village Other,* and author of the following books: *Poems from Oklahoma* (Hesperidian Press, 1962); *The Blood Letting* (Renegade Press, 1963) and *The Commanche Cantos* (Sign of the Gun Press, 1965). His work has appeared in *El Corno Emplumado, Yale Literary Magazine* and other publications. "Poems *from Oklahoma* (Hesperidian Press, 1962); *The Blood Letting*

Bob Kaufman lives in San Francisco. He is one of the founders of the magazine *Beatitude.* His *Abomunist Manifesto* was published in 1959 by City Lights. "Benediction" is from his book, *Solitudes Crowded with Loneliness.*

Joel Kohut was born in 1940 in New York. His work has appeared in *Destine, Orphee, Moska, Ascent* and *Nihilist.*

Tuli Kupferberg was born in 1923 in New York City. His poems have appeared in *Yugen, Fuck-You* and *New York Herald Tribune.* He is the author of *The Book of the Body* (Birth Press, 1966); *1001 Ways to Beat the Draft* (with Robert Bashlow. Oliver Layton Press, 1966) and *Caught in the Act* (Birth Press, 1966). "Flower Passion" was published in *Wormwood Review,* 17.

Peter La Farge was born in Santa Fe, New Mexico; died in New York a week after contributing to a recording for a record of this book. Widely known as a folksong composer specializing in Indian themes, he described himself for these notes as follows: "Peter La Farge avoided being a poet until his poems outnumbered him with the wrath of unused talents—24 prize-fights, 10 years in rodeo, 6 record albums—now home at last—poet." His poem "Autumn 1964" appeared in *Broadside.*

Carl Larsen, born in 1935 in Hermosa Beach, California, has had 250 poems and stories published in various magazines. A novel, *The Book of Eric Hammerscoffer,* is in preparation at

Poet's Press, Washington, D. C. His first book is *The Plot to Assassinate the Chase National Bank* (New York, 7 Poet's Press, 1961).

Julius Lester was born in 1939 in St. Louis, and is now a full-time SNCC worker based in Atlanta. Widely known as a folk-singer and composer, he has co-authored with Pete Seeger "The 12-String Guitar as Played by Leadbelly" (Oak, New York, 1965). His essays have appeared in *Sing Out* and *Broadside*.

D. A. Levy was born in 1942 in Cleveland, Ohio. His work has appeared in *El Corno Emplumado, Vincent, Smorgasbrain, Tlaloc* (England), *Entrails* and many other publications. He is the author of the following books: *R. E. Visions* (Niagara Press Today,1966); *Cleveland Undercovers* (7 Flowers Press, Cleveland, 1966); *Kibbutz in the Sky* (7 Flowers Press, Cleveland, (1967); *North American Book of the Dead* (7 Flowers Press, 1966) and *The Egyptian Stroboscope* (with D. R. Wagner) (7 Flowers Press, 1966-7). He died in 1969. "Ode to Mayor Locker" first appeared in *The Marrawhannah Quarterly*.

Bruce Lippincott, born in 1924 in Philadelphia, now lives in Santa Fe, New Mexico. He is a tenor saxophonist and was musical director for the first poetry and jazz sessions at *The Cellar* in San Francisco (recorded on Fantasy). His work has been published in *Beatitude*.

Worth Long, born in 1936 in North Carolina, is now living in Atlanta, where he is an active worker in SNCC. His poems have appeared in *New South, Umbra, Harvard Advocate,* and other publications. "Safari" appeared in *The Harvard Crimson,* Summer, 1964.

Clarence Major was born in Atlanta in 1936; he is now living in New York. Stories, poems and articles have appeared in many magazines, including: *Negro Digest, Entrails, Human Voice*

Quarterly, Black Dialogue, and in the anthology, *Where Is Viet Nam? American Poets Respond.* A book of his poems will be published by Olivant Press, Homestead, Florida, and another is in preparation entitled *Swallow the Lake,* from which "American Setup" is taken.

Clive Matson was born in 1941 in Los Angeles. His work has appeared in *Intrepid #5, The Floating Bear, The Great Society, Grist, In New York* and *Down Here.* His book *Mainline to the Heart* was published in 1966 by the Poets Press.

David Meltzer was born in 1937 in New York; he now lives in San Francisco. His poems have appeared in *Big Table, Yugen, Coyote's Journal, Yale Literary Magazine* and others. He is author of *Poems* (1959); *Regas* (1959); *The Clown* (1959); *We All Have Something to Say* (1962) and *The Process* (1965). His poem "Dances" first appeared in *Regas* (Discovery Books, S. F., 1959).

June Meyer was bron in 1936 in Harlem, New York. She has been published in: *Esquire, Mademoiselle, The Nation, American Dialog* and the *Liberator.*

George Montgomery was born in 1938 in Jersey City, New Jersey. His poems have appeared in *Kauri, London Observer, East Village Other, Floating Bear* and other publications. He is the author of two books: *Mary Jane Papers* (7 Flowers Press, Cleveland, Ohio, 1966) and *Moonblood* (Vincent Press, 1967).

John Morgan was born in 1946 in Tennessee. His poems have appeared in *Kauri.* As a Marine Corps Lance Corporal he attracted national attention when he told a peace rally in New York that he had gone AWOL rather than fight in Vietnam. "Second Coming" appeared in *Kauri.*

Freda Norton was born in 1935 in Houston, Texas. She paints under the name of Frieda Pointer and has several paintings in the Sam Houston State Museum. Her poetry has appeared in *New Lantern, Club Review, Coercion* and *Kauri.*

Joel Oppenheimer was born in 1930, in Yonkers, N. Y. He is a playwright and printer as well as poet, and is now directing the St. Mark's Church cultural program in N. Y. He was one of the Black Mountain group of poets and has been widely published. His recent books include *The Dutiful Son* and *The Love Bit.*

Marge Piercy was born in 1936 in Detroit. A part of her first novel *Maud Awake* is appearing in an anthology of New Women Writers. Her poems have appeared in the *Transatlantic Review, Fiddlehead, Chelsea* and other magazines. "Visit to a Dead Man on a Summer Day" appeared in *Charleton Miscellany* (Winter, 1967).

Alan Planz was born in 1937 in New York. He has been published in a number of magazines, including *Poetry, Massachusetts Review, The Nation* and *Yugen.* He is co-editor of an anthology of poems on civil rights.

N. H. Pritchard was born in New York in 1939. His work has been published in *Umbra, Literary Review, Freedomways, East Village Other* and *Poetry Northwest.* He has participated in many readings.

Margaret Randall is a native New Yorker now living in Mexico City, where she and her husband edit *El Corno Emplumado.* Her work has appeared in many magazines, including: *Liberation, Nomad, Duende, Provincetown Review, The Outsider.* Her recent books include: *Giant of Tears* and *Ectasy Is a Number.*

Lennox Raphael was born in 1939 and lives in New York. His work has appeared in publications in Latin America, Europe, the Caribbean and the United States, including *American Dialog.*

David Rasey, born in 1935 in Nebraska, is the author of two collections of poems: *Subways* (Renegade Press, 1964) and *The Artist* (The Second Renaissance Press, 1964). His work has appeared in the *New Lantern Club Review, Beginning, Kauri, Eight Pager* and other magazines.

Ishmael Reed was born in Tennessee in 1938, and is now working in New York as a novelist and teacher. His poems have appeared in *East Village Other, Mainstream, Liberator* and other publications.

Steven Richmond was born in 1941 in Los Angeles. He has published two books of poems; *Hitler Painted Roses* and *Poems.* His work has appeared in *Entrails, Ole, Wormwood Review, Notes from Underground* and *The Marrawhanna Quarterly.*

Sonia Sanchez was born in 1935 in Birmingham, Alabama. Her poems have appeared in *Liberator, Negro Digest, Afro-American, Revolution, For Malcolm: Poems of His Life and Death* and other magazines. "Summary" appeared in the *Transatlantic Review* #22 (Autumn 1966).

Ed Sanders was born in 1939 and is active in the New York poetry and song scene. He is a co-founder of The Fugs, and editor of *Fuck-You, a Magazine of the Arts.* "Poem from Jail" is from the book by that title published by City Lights, San Francisco, 1963.

Dan Saxon was born in 1939 in New York City. He is the author of two books: *Absence* (1962) and *In the Shower and Out of It* (1966). His poems have appeared in many magazines, including *Intrepid, Wormwood, Lines, Kauri, Yowl* and *Poets at Le Metro.* "Atman" appeared in the *University of Tampa Review.*

Fred Silber was born in New York City in 1952. This is his first published poem.

Isiah Smith was born in 1939 in Morgan City, Louisiana. "Church on the Corner of Union and Third" first appeared in *Magazine—2*, 1965.

Clee Snipe, Jr., was born in 1938 in Orangeburg, South Carolina. He is currently working with American Friends Group in their Remedial Reading Program in East Harlem.

Jane Stembridge was born in Georgia in 1939 and has been active in the Southern civil rights movement. Her poems have appeared in *The Student Voice, Liberation* and other publications. "I Play Flute" appeared in her book by the same title (Flute Publications, Tougaloo, Miss., 1966).

Ronald Stone, a Kentuckian, born in 1937, has worked as an actor, laborer, social worker, school teacher and poet-in-residence at the Crows Toe Coffee House in Washington, D.C. He has published in *American Weave, Soul Book* and other magazines.

Gloria Tropp, singer, poet, designer and composer, is a New Yorker whose poems have appeared in *Bluebeat, Theo, Intrepid* and other magazines. "Poem for Ernie Henry" appeared in *Intrepid #4.*

Stephen Tropp, a native of Vienna, is a New Yorker whose book of poems, *Mozart in Hell,* was published in 1959. His poems have appeared in *Exodus, Birth, Yugen, Beat Coast East* and other magazines. "To Jackie in Jail" appeared in *Intrepid #4.*

Diane Wakoski was born in 1937 in California and is now living in New York. She appeared in *Four Young Lady Poets* (Totem Corinth, New York, 1962) and is the author of *Coins and Coffins* (1962) and *Discrepancies and Apparitions* (Doubleday, New York, 1965). She has published in *El Corno Emplumado, Art and Literature, Riverrun, Vincent* and many other magazines.

William Wantling was born in 1933 in Peoria, Illinois. He has appeared in many magazines and has published: *Search* (Crank Books, N.Y., 1963); *Machine & Destiny* (Hors Commerce Press, 1964); *Five Poem Songs* (Hors Commerce Press, 1964); *Head First* (Erik Kiviat, New York, 1965); *Down, Off & Out* (Mimeo Press, Chicago, 1965); *The Source* (Dustbooks, San Francisco, 1966) and *The Awakening* (Turret, London, 1967). "Poetry" is from *From the Jungle's Edge,* 1967.

ABOUT THE EDITOR

WALTER LOWENFELS is the editor of *Walt Whitman's Civil War* (N.Y., 1961; *Poets of Today* (N.Y., 1964); *Where Is Vietnam? American Poets Respond* (N.Y., 1967) and *The Writing on the Wall* (N.Y., 1969). He is the author of a prose work: *To An Imaginary Daughter* (N.Y., 1964), and has the following volumes of poetry in print: *Some Deaths* (Highlands, N.C., 1964); *Land of Roseberries* (Mexico City, 1965); *Translations from Scorpius* (Monmouth, Maine, 1966). A prose book, *The Poetry of My Politics,* and *The Portable Walter,* a selection of his own prose and verse, edited by Robert Gover, were recently published.

Mr. Lowenfels is associate editor of the magazine *American Dialog,* the father of four children and grandfather of twelve, and is now living in Peekskill, New York, with his wife, Lillian.

Twenty-one of the poets in *In a Time of Revolution* have read their poems in a record, *New Jazz Poets,* edited by Lowenfels and released recently by Broadside Records, N.Y.

VINTAGE POLITICAL SCIENCE
AND SOCIAL CRITICISM

A free catalogue of VINTAGE BOOKS *will be sent at your request. Write to* Vintage Books, 457 Madison Avenue, New York, New York 10022.

A free catalogue of VINTAGE BOOKS *will be sent at your request.* Write to Vintage Books, 457 Madison Avenue, New York, New York 10022.

VINTAGE BELLES-LETTRES

A free catalogue of VINTAGE BOOKS *will be sent at your request. Write to* Vintage Books, 457 Madison Avenue, New York, New York 10022.

A free catalogue of VINTAGE BOOKS *will be sent at your request. Write to* Vintage Books, 457 Madison Avenue, New York, New York 10022.

VINTAGE WORKS OF SCIENCE
AND PSYCHOLOGY

VINTAGE HISTORY—WORLD

VINTAGE BIOGRAPHY AND AUTOBIOGRAPHY

A free catalogue of VINTAGE BOOKS *will be sent at your request. Write to* Vintage Books, 457 Madison Avenue, New York, New York 10022.